looking at city planning

Le Corbusier
looking at city planning

translated from the french by eleanor levieux
an orion press book
grossman publishers · new york 1971

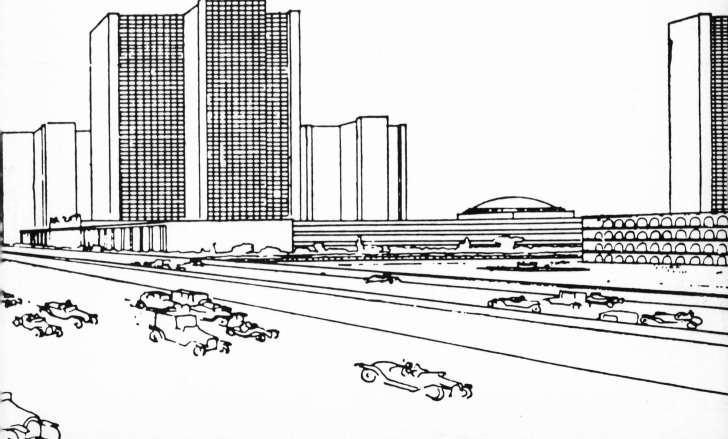

CONTENTS

iNTRodUCTioN

In the space of only three-quarters of a century a brutal rupture, unlike anything in the annals of history, has wrenched all of the social life of the West from its framework, which was relatively traditional and remarkably in harmony with geography.

The explosive, the cause of the rupture, was the sudden intrusion of speed into a life which until then had kept time to the step of horses' hooves—speed in production, speed in the transportation of people and things. Speed appears and the big cities burst or suffocate, the rural regions are depopulated, each province is violated in its most intimate heart. The two traditional types of human settlement (city and village) go through a terrible crisis. Our cities spread shapelessly, indefinitely. The city, coherent urban organism, disappears; the village, coherent rural organism, bears the stigmata of ever-faster decay. Abruptly thrown into contact with the big city, the village loses its balance and is deserted.

Drunk on speed and movement, all of society seems to have begun, unconsciously, to revolve around itself like an airplane caught in denser and denser fog and going into a dizzy spin. The only way out of that drunkenness is catastrophe—a nose dive and then a crash.

Pivotal centers of concentration and redistribution, the trading cities are located at the points of intersection of the major thoroughfares. They occupy the sites which have always been marked out for them, for the roads follow the flow of water, the *Thalweg*. First came the footpath, then parallel, the trail for horses and donkeys. Canals, railway tracks, kings' highways, today's motorways all follow the same path, as it were. And at certain points, they too marked out by fate, two roads meet; sometimes more. Outstanding, predestined points, places of concentration, centers of dispersion. It is at these intersections that the trading cities grew up: market towns, county seats, larger cities, capitals, etc. In these focal points along human thoroughfares, the merchants gathered and with them, their bankers. And also those who exchange ideas, the scholars and the teachers, and also those who express life where it appears to be most lively, the artists. Authority quite naturally grows up in a radio-concentric place.

Mechanically produced speed unleashed industry, which, actively and without stopping to think, grew up in these already existing sites because they offered lodging, food and a labor force, in addition to the countless social resources that any concentration of human beings always offers. The gigantic overflowing of the first machine-age cycle brought these cities to their point of congestion.

The radio-concentric industrial city fails. It molests men, imposing frenzied daily patterns of mechanized traffic, and making a congested jumble of places of work and dwelling places—successive encircling choking belts, interpenetrating one another like gears, belts of industrial sites and belts of rented housing, workshops and suburbs, inner suburbs and outlying suburbs. Population figures have swelled: four and a half million inhabitants in Paris, eleven million in London, eight to ten million in New York. The public transport networks are always kept up to date so that every day the masses can keep on flowing into the city, by subway, bus, suburban train or highway. Every day, everything is rectified, coordinated, perfected, but at man's expense, at the cost of his unhappiness. His solar day of twenty-four hours manifests no tenderness toward him; he lives artificially, dangerously. Natural conditions have been wiped out. The modern industrial radio-concentric city is a flourishing cancer!

Embarrackment and inhumanity are what characterize our poorly sound-proofed rent boxes, with the street on their doorsteps, the street with its ruckus and its mechanized terror, the mortal enemy of children. Many people think they can make up for the nervous wear-and-tear and the myriad unpleasantness of the city by living in little houses on the outskirts. The need they feel to escape is legitimate; a rejection of the conditions which are current in our cities today is at the very root of a doctrine shared by all of the great contemporary architects. But how does this escape work out in fact? By the anarchic proliferation (pseudo-escape!) of little cities nibbling away at nature and defacing the handsome rural communities; by the dizzying expense (public transportation, complicated system of roads, utility mains, postal services, etc.) to which the government is compelled by the unwholesome swelling of our cities. This wastage on a gigantic scale, this disorganization of the urban phenomenon constitutes one of the most crushing burdens that modern society has to bear.

One half the fruits of the effort made by the general public is snatched away by the government to pay for this waste. If people occupied in a rational way the territory in which they live, they would not have to work more than one half as much.

Of course the little house ("my house," "my very own home"), flanked by its fruit and vegetable garden and its sheltering tree, fills the hearts and the minds of the crowd; which is why businessmen can make substantial profits by dividing the land into lots, manufacturing doors and windows, building roads complete with utility mains, making the trams, buses, subways, automobiles, bicycles, and motorcycles that are necessary if the Virgilian dream is to come true.

The little house crushes the mistress of the house under the burden of domestic chores and crushes the financial resources of the township under the burden of upkeep. What does remain, however, to the credit of the family house is the valid and even sacred notion of family unity seeking re-immersion in "natural conditions."

Those natural conditions are inscribed on one of the Tables of the Law of contemporary city planning, which relies upon three materials: pure air, sun, and greenery. But the other Table reminds us that the solar cycle is short: twenty-four fateful hours regulate the activity of men by setting the limit of feasibility on their comings and goings. Any attempt at city planning must be measured against this law of twenty-four hours. Loud and clear, those who foment "garden cities" and cause the disjointedness of the cities proclaimed: every man his own little garden, his own little house, his freedom guaranteed. They were lying—taking advantage of the trust placed in them! The day is only twenty-four hours long. The day is inadequate. "In contrast to this great panicky dispersal, a natural law must be called to mind: men like to form groups so as to help and defend one another and to economize their efforts. If they scatter, as they are doing today, to separate housing lots, this means the city is sick, hostile, no longer fulfills its functions."

How can these two axioms be reconciled? How can we find a remedy for a scandalous waste of time while, simultaneously, making sure that "nature is written into the lease"? How can we prevent our cities from spreading so far that they become diluted, losing their form and their soul? We propose to deal with all of these questions together in this book.

looking at city planning

CHAPTER 1
The year 1943 and the years that followed

1943—a year with nothing special about it, situated perhaps at the point of inflexion between the sum of the errors made and the dawn of a new start.

We must be clearly aware of the reality of the problem that concerns us here: building. The art of building was still tied by teaching methods to the manual agility and mental patterns of the past; still acknowledging full rights to the Greco-Roman "styles," it was torn between two groups of pretenders: those who call themselves *architects* and those who are called *engineers,* and this art of building was nothing more, in the public opinion and in the opinion of popular leaders, than a tangled issue, a vipers' nest, a Gordian knot. The Gordian knot shall be cut by a keen-edged weapon wielded by a veritable army of weapon-bearers named *builders.* That army decides the issue. Once this is done, this term, which actually covers a whole program, rallies, gathers, unites, puts in order and produces. All themes, taken as a whole, are penetrated by unity and continuity. Nothing is contradictory any longer. The builder is present at the place of manufacture as well as on the scaffolding at the temple; he is the reasoning and ingenious mind as well as the poet. Everyone in his place, all in orderly hierarchical ranks.

The city planner is nothing other than the architect. The city planner organizes architectural space, determines the place and purpose of the containing vessels which are built, and links all these things in time and in space by a circulatory network. And the other man, the architect, concerned for instance with a mere dwelling place and, within that dwelling with a mere kitchen, likewise erects containers, creates spaces, determines the paths of circulation. In terms of the creative act, the architect and the city planner are one and the same.

There are eight thousand architects in France, and only a few city planners. And even at best, the city planning they practice is still not full-fledged; it is retrospective rather, museographic, mimetic, and very specifically concerned with decor—with decor as ornament, the raiment of a country, city or town, raiment which has nothing to do with season but with dramatic display.

And yet great city planners have gone before, but they wielded ideas, not pencils — Balzac, Fourier, Considérant, Proudhon . . . As much as one hundred years ago, at the birth of the machine age, in Paris, Balzac had breathed in the macerating stench of the centuries accumulated in a vat hugged tight by its walls: the city. The others had expanded their lungs to the breeze blowing off the open sea of imagination; they had felt, thought and phrased, and this produced a prophecy on which the surge of ingrained habits and immediate interests came crashing down. Then everything was swept bare. Other men came back, meditated in turn (from other premises) and, prophesying in turn, were smothered in another surge of habits and interests. And so it went, again and again . . . the effort of each succeeding generation. A stupefying event thrust its summits into the sky, launched its huge crests toward the horizons; something genuinely serious, profound, intimate and general was happening: the machine-age civilization was born. Bitter fruits: the great modern wars, those destroyers of tranquillity, those instruments of adventure that tear away and uproot, leave rubble, institute the tragedies of tomorrow, appeal to the genius of men so that life will not be extinguished in those so-very-brief periods which are sometimes all that is offered to society and which suffice to cause death from starvation, cold or despair.

So brief a period calls for adequate wisdom, firmness and lucidity in decision. Chance and improvisation are tools too clumsy for the quality of work needed in order to install a machine-age civilization and equip it in an appropriate and technical way. So many things will have to be envisaged, planned, got off to a start within brief instants and in so many corners of the country — a genuine, disturbing symphony bringing city men and country dwellers into tune — that there has to be a line of conduct, at all costs. The doctrine that is needed must be neither too heavily nor too lightly mapped out, since it is necessary and must be sufficient.

What happened at the time of the great surprise — the defeat in 1940? An instinctive, understandable movement of withdrawal, a renewal of contact with . . . something solid. Where is solidity to be found at the very hour of catastrophe if not in the reflexes which are the maturity of earlier meditation? And so we touched our feet down and our hands down on that which had existed, in order to lean on something, "get our footing again." Once we had done that, and once we had given more thought to what we are (men), who we are (Frenchmen), what we know how to do and can do (technicians), and what we want (reach up to the joy of living), we found that we were divided into those two fundamental human groups: the active and the passive. And into two other human groups: the selfless and the selfish. And under the influence of the two poles of sensitivity: the imaginative and the conformists, the poets and the dullards.

Yet there is no lack of talent; it is more abundant in France than elsewhere. But in the past few decades, the country has suffered from atrophy of will power; as a result it is no longer guided by taste, and that is greatly to the advantage of bad taste. Where other countries simply haven't any taste at all, France has begun to cultivate bad taste. Teaching is one large contributing factor to that situation; it has tried to make us believe that the taste of times past can be used today, that we need only make imitations.

Even now, the divergence is still between tomorrow and yesterday. Many of the people who take the floor in this discussion are only journalists, sometimes talented writers, often businessmen. At a time when city planning needs to start from scratch, many people who are not city planners themselves would like to persuade the public at large.

And yet, in waves, successively, over the three years 1941, 1942, 1943, people were set to work, architects made responsible for drawing up plans for the reconstruction of the cities, the towns and the villages. In this way they got their hand in — into architecture — and had a taste of city planning and, becoming by doing, they entered into the realm of city planning.

For the time being, nothing very specific as to deadlines, prices or efficiency. Euphoria or the end of a truce. But tomorrow, to the trumpet sound of work getting under way (materials, labor, transportation, cost and time, and service rendered) once again the situation will be like the fighting on the battlefronts: Germany or America, industry and trade out for the kill, the kill being France; France which had thought it could base its reconstruction on its (non-existent) army of craftsmen, on a sentimental program placed (or which would be placed) barrier-wise across the path of real needs, outside of the realities and the possibilities of life.

Provided a coherent doctrine emerges in time, perhaps all these new professional city planners will find it shedding light enough to indicate the direction they should go in.

Common sense will be able to get a grip on itself once that other battle has begun, the new and violent battle of reconstruction. The solution to the real problem—*living today!*—will be found in the intense effort made by the entire country and the passionate participation of those who will be its leaders: the architects who have become city planners.

Once again there will be lines drawn on paper, once again blueprints. But this time, work done with a clear vision.

CHAPTER 2

The technical viewpoint—the spiritual viewpoint—the solidarity between them

Rather than continuing to bandy words about and constantly contrasting different points of view, it would be better to bring them together in a reasonable and harmonious order.

The technical viewpoint does not contradict the spiritual viewpoint; the one is the raw material while the other is the foreman in charge. The one cannot survive without the other.

Technology — raw material in its most inert form — represents, first of all, the sum of all of the innocent, spontaneous, naive and unrelated inventions born of chance or in the laboratories; then, secondly, it is the unlimited procession toward an equally unlimited goal which leads things to unexpected and sometimes overwhelming outcomes. There is no such thing as a minor or a major invention; there are only minor or major consequences. Gunpowder and printing were enough to turn one of the great pages in human history.

First steam, then electricity and the combustion engine multiplied the power of the biceps or the harnessed team enormously, opening the way for the machine-age civilization. Just how far will power expand? When will it reach its levelling-off point? Money interests or spiritual interests have taken over the minor or major inventions: turmoil in industrial manufacturing, or the hesitations of always reticent customers. The day will come when, on this particular point, for instance, the harvest will be ripe: the railways (which had fomented the machine-age civilization) will be supplanted by the highways for travel over short distances and by airplanes (they are being got ready now) for long distances.

Interests are as varied as needs. Stomach, sex and head lay down the programs and so decide whether the original inventions will be a financial or moral success. In principle, as indeed in fact, there is hardly ever any connection between the inventor and success. A battlefield stretches between them and on it can be seen in action the passions and the consequences of those passions, the grandeur and the littleness of the human act.

Inventions are the raw material, the condition on which all life depends. And so the question arises very clearly: whether or not to possess the raw material; whether to possess a little or a lot of it; hasten to gather quantities of it in order to use it or negligently overlook it? But another idea is also being put forward today in certain quarters, the idea of striving mightily to reject the inventions, removing the raw material far far away from our undertakings.

Because, in fact, by behaving falsely — weakness, lack of courage, slothful imagination — some parties are trying to place roadblocks in the way of inventions (so that they won't disturb anything; rather, to make their disturbances cease, and cease so completely that it is eliminated and the bygone days come back decorated, by this quirk of reasoning, with exceptionally attractive features). In order to turn the trick, the spiritual element has been drafted into battle and dubbed the enemy of technology. Sensitivity has been appealed to, and people have demonstrated that it has been mistreated, disturbed, traumatized by the products of technomania. They have been billed as enemies: technology versus sensitivity, technology versus spirituality. And warnings have been issued to the country at large, to public opinion, to the public heart. They have launched a crusade. Whereas it was actually interests of all sorts that were at stake (in the shadow of laziness), the debate was couched in terms of God and the Devil — spiritual struggling to overthrow material concerns. And when came, pathetic, the time for great decisions, when a civilization had the opportunity to make a grand start toward harmonious destinies, the machine was sabotaged.

And yet the reality is positive, for whoever wants to see it.

Techniques have broadened the reach of poetry. They have not shrunk horizons, doomed the wide open spaces or put the poets in prison. Instead, the precision of the measuring instruments they use has opened up the spaces before us to a fantastic extent — and so, has opened the way to dreams: the stellar worlds and the dizzying depths of life on this earth of ours. Every minute, dreams and poetry burst out of this technical progress. So, the problem does not lie there.

An artificial world of the mind has been created. In it, the mind, weary of the joys of invention and creation, has found fulfillment only in the cult of recollection. Recollections whose substance has been distorted . . . things purposely recalled so that they would be perpetuated or would at least come back to imprint themselves on our lives, taking on the value of imperishable acquisitions. Whereas in fact, when they first appeared, they had been unforeseen inventions, and even then they had upset the established order and cherished habits. Starting with words, you fashion things whose meaning and shape are arbitrarily determined and immobilized, a glossary of terms harking back to the most permanent notions but which are frozen in the most immutable postures: roof, village, steeple, house, etc.; stone, wood and earth; hands, heart and soul; fatherland, hearth. And thanks to these things, the modern world will not get by.

As an example, take this meaningful analysis. The scientists, with their measuring instruments and their research, have shown us that rocks are made up of the billions of beings that used to live in the seas. Each of those living beings was a dazzling sample of harmonious forms; some of them piled up one million or even ten million deep to make a single cubic millimeter of rock! Another of those once living rocks constitutes what, in Paris, the quarriers have called "the royal bank." Elsewhere, fragmented or raised up by geological accidents, they formed the magnificent site, the archetypal "eternal" horizon. The stone taken from it was used to build the houses and the walls edging roads and enclosing vineyards. An imperative, binding link, people called it, the affiliation between this site and these walls, these houses, these hearths, these men, this tradition, this duty . . . Then innocently, the scientist comes along and tells you that, upon closer examination, he finds that that rock was born three hundred million years ago, in the unfathomable depths ten thousand meters below the surface of the sea, so that those austere mountains, those noble silhouettes standing out so clearly against the blue sky are really portions of the sea bottom which were victims of some accident or other . . .

The lesson to be drawn is not that this rock is linked by divine right to that house, but, in much more eloquent terms, that these rocks which we find beautiful are a miracle of cellular composition, veritable microscopic limestone palaces cemented with silica. And that nature is organization in all things, from the infinitely large to the infinitely small. And that the heart of man will be comforted and his mind reassured once he has, through his creations, brought himself into harmony with the universe, with the laws of nature wherein all is birth, growth, death and eternal renewal.

The technological viewpoint is not the adversary of the spiritual, but, instead, one of its acute forms, expressing the absolute side of reasoning, logical deductions and pre-ordained mathematical or geometrical results. The spiritual viewpoint is more detached from facts, experience and the reality of matter. By virtue of its efforts to judge, evaluate, measure "in relationship to" (in relation to us, to the human element), it is closer to consciousness. Life naturally follows its course in between those two poles, in an atmosphere of continuity, contiguity, succession, contact, not in an atmosphere of rupture; in agreement and not in opposition.

From the relationships just outlined two common-sense decisions can be formulated, decisions channelled by courage and joyous action as well:

1) An appeal to all of the powers of technology to constitute a set of tools suited to the new step that mankind has taken.

When the alternative is between yes and no, choose *yes*, and you choose the dazzling certainty of attaining goals as yet unknown but which harmoniously express the deep-lying present realities. Goals unknown and therefore to be created, themes of a great conquest, source therefore of creative joy.

Say "No," and you make the contradictory effort, fighting against the natural current of life, the effort of trying to suspend the course of events, you choose the illusion of clinging to things which have already been eclipsed by the present moment. Say "No," and you prevent modern society from living in time to its own rhythm, achieving its equilibrium, and consequently you maintain inefficiency and inadequacy; you leave current cases of disequilibrium hanging in mid-air, along with their social problems and the whole procession of menaces harking back to spiritual values.

2) An appeal to the values which are human, first of all, and only afterwards national, regional or local. The wish to live otherwise than in an equivocal climate so generalized as to overwhelm the day-to-day gestures of all, to live in a quest for the joy of living—the only

genuine goal to set any civilization—that wish is worldwide, universal. There, in that wish, is where the problem lies. The individual is summoned by an obligation to carry out a molecular reform of the modern world. Spiritual currents encounter one another in the wave-filled atmosphere and join forces in the radio sets in each individual home. Thought is worldwide; the convergence of spiritual powers in the quest for wisdom is indispensable. China and India as well can contribute the special quality of their message to those who might, perhaps, tend to be too caught up in the demands of common sense or material awareness alone.

All of the resources of technology and all of the spiritual values deployed coherently, contiguously, and all fanning out from the center which is our sole concern, from man, corporeal man and spiritual man (the man who reasons and the man who intuits)—that is the much-to-be-hoped-for solution of an absurd conflict between the technological and the spiritual points of view.

CHAPTER 3

A NEW MACHINE AGE SOCIETY

The nineteenth century ushered in an era of arithmetic, of experimental and applied science.

Machines appeared in a massive way. The number of machines increased so much that habits, customs were upset and altered, and since then, the economy and the social sciences have continually undergone more and more profound transformations, clues to the decisive disturbances that are in the offing.

Fully a hundred years ago, the first locomotive pulled a freight train along the rails between two cities and thereby inserted into relationships and into the transportation phenomenon a change in duration—actually an element of speed which was destined to increase all the time, extending its effects to the whole of human activities.

For thousands of years, those activities had been timed on the basis of about 3 miles per hour, the rate of which man, horse and ox were capable. From now on, in contrast to that cadence, we must adjust ourselves to the 30 to 60 miles per hour covered by ships or by automobiles on smooth roads, the 200 or 300 miles per hour at which airplanes travel, and the immeasurable speeds of telegraph, telephone and radio.

The consequences were not long in coming. Men and their thoughts were gripped by an intense agitation, the same which also drew goods and raw materials into a new circuit. The limits of what could be demanded and also of what could be controlled were stretched beyond belief. A new rhythm destroying age-old habits and forging new attitudes. When we say attitudes, here, we are thinking especially of working conditions and leisure conditions, inserted into a pre-ordained unit of measurement: the twenty-four hour cycle of the solar day which will always and forever determine the rhythm of mankind's activities.

Family traditions were upset, and social relationships as well.

Perfected machines made printing the universal vehicle of thought, available to every member of society—ideas and pictures, science, art, history and geography, economics and politics. Soon the transmission of ideas was seconded by an invaluable device: the photographic document, both still and in motion.

From then on knowledge took on unheard of, even revealing forms, detailed, multiplied, multi-geared, carrying the conviction of the absolute: the document. At the same time, it went democratic, spreading indefinitely through the use of machines, irrespective of previous limits or castes. For thousands of years, man had lived within the universe defined by a radius of ten or twelve miles around his place of shelter; but today, he can read about or view the entire world:

     —geography (sites, flora and fauna, harvests and industrial products);

     —human races, as tallied by the illustrated document, the documentary film. They are revealed to us in detail, their appearance, their customs, what they build;

     —climates from one pole to the other, by way of the tropics and the equator, and from sea level to the highest altitudes.

Such an abundance of information means so many inducements to greed, and also so much encouragement of self-centered withdrawal.

The effect of this broadening of the horizons was to make the thirst for knowledge, analysis and observation singularly keener. The first reaction against it was anxiety, fear in the face of something new. The response to this was to investigate the past in order to find some reassurance. Archaeology was supreme, reigning over all teaching. It was an invitation to a refusal to create, to loss of the *taste for creating*—taste for, joy in the *risk* of, creating.

Trade and industry developed at a rate far exceeding any forecasts—influx of materials and equipment; relinquishment of manual methods; edifying and undeniable virtue of *precise* industrial products, etc. . . . In their haste to improvise, industries arbitrarily formed concentrations, swelling the existing population centers to an enormous degree; and meanwhile—and precisely for that reason—the land was abandoned increasingly, as industry recruited an ever-growing labor force.

Electricity having got the better of the night (and so eliminated an age-old norm), the cities seemed to deck themselves with such dazzling charms that the fated exodus from the country became the headlong rush to the big city. Universal history. Worldwide event.

Handicrafts were replaced by industry, and the craftsman by the machine with its accompanying industrial worker or unskilled laborer. The unity of the family was wounded as the father, the mother sometimes, the daughter, the son each went his separate way each morning to some breadwinning job, each living his own adventure, sometimes forming a violent contrast with the others. The rupture in the traditional foundations of human relationships, built on confidence, is made clear by this observation of decisive importance: the person who consumes today no longer knows the person who produces. Nothing of what was formerly a yardstick can be used today to evaluate the behavior of a society wrenched away from its traditions and having taken its first steps in the unknown reaches of a new machine-age civilization.

The architectual revolution that takes place

The locomotive, the nineteenth-century book with its increasingly accurate photo-reproduction processes, bring a prodigious flood of documents, like so much food tossed to whoever wants it. All of the places and all the objects that have been built through all the ages. Under such an avalanche of suggestions, the line of evolution was broken—that age-old line derived from Mediterranean antiquity, from the revolutionary Middle Ages, and from certain average adaptations which emerged from the classical era. The techniques used had remained constant: stone, brick and wood. Then suddenly they ceased to be used, replaced by steel sections, glass, reinforced concrete, and the scientific methods of calculating strength based, insofar as possible, on the safeness of artificial materials of constant quality: steels and binding materials.

Specialized schools were founded for the purpose of training engineers in the new sciences. Everything was sounded out, looked into; curiosity and inventiveness were in the place of honor. Applied science made a prodigious leap ahead. Automobiles and airplanes embodied the new speeds. Radio wrapped the earth around in its countless waves which, tirelessly picked up on receiving sets, were the vehicle of every kind of thought, every slogan: the event snowballing, traveling on its own momentum. And soon man is overwhelmed by so much newness, crushed even under his discoveries, society divided into hostile classes, individuals bruised or hindered in their day-to-day behavior.

People moved away from the human viewpoint. It was left behind, forgotten even, lost. Heedlessness, abandonment of the awareness of things; exaggeration; grandeur and puerility. Machines turned an unsuspected page of human history and, because man let himself be taken by surprise, mistreated in the course of this first hundred-year cycle of the machine age, some people refuse to acknowledge the place which in truth machines do occupy. They even try to deny them! Now, when it comes to building, the effect of the scientific discoveries is decisive, expressed in a handful of fundamentally revolutionary stages in the construction process.

1) Separation of the carrying functions (posts and beams) from the parts that are carried (wall fillings or partitions); the skeleton (of steel or reinforced concrete) is independent; it goes down under the ground to find its support without the help of the traditional foundation walls.

2) The façade, since it no longer has any compulsory carrying function, can be considered a mere membrane between the outside and the inside. It no longer receives the weight of the flooring and, under these circumstances, it suddenly offers a complete solution to the centuries-long effort to bring the maximum amount of light into buildings. As much as 100% of the surface of the façade can now be a glass wall.

3) Since the structure's independent skeleton is in contact with the ground only through a small number of supporting points (posts), the elimination of all underpinnings becomes possible, thus leaving the area under the building free. This available space can be assigned specific purposes, particularly that of solving certain traffic problems (today's hopeless dead end of two tangled types of traffic, automobile and pedestrian, two categories of speed, 60 miles per hour and 3 miles per hour).

4) Wooden roof beams can be replaced by reinforced concrete terraces which, being horizontal, will lend themselves, in addition, to certain worthwhile installations.

5) Inside the structure, with the exception of a few widely-spaced posts, the floor plan is altogether free, since the vertical separations (partition walls) no longer need to be directly above one another from one floor to the next, as required until now by the practice of having carrying walls.

And there you have, in a brief outline, the basis of the architectural revolution which has been carried out to date through the use of modern techniques. *It is important.*

There can be no doubt that enormous advantages are now available to the architect and the city planner who have to solve a series of problems brought about, precisely, by the inventions made in this last century of technology.

The architectural revolution which has been carried out offers its resources for the benefit of planning contemporary cities. . . .

Just as a reference, let's list a few of the recent achievements that bring invaluable means within our grasp.

In the USA, the height of buildings rose rapidly in two decades from 300 to 1000 feet. From this development stemmed an entirely new technique, using concrete and steel, as well as fire-prevention methods. Other corollaries: the perfect mechanism of vertical mechanical systems of circulation; the distribution of conditioned air in large buildings as well as in railway cars or steamboats, in the tunnels below the Hudson River or in commercial aircraft. The conquest of height brings with it the solution to essential problems involved in the planning of modern cities, to wit: the possibility of reinstating *natural conditions* (sun, space, greenery); the separation of pedestrian from automobile; the creation of qualified arrangements we can call "extensions of the dwelling" by which to reserve a new fate to child-care and eugenics and offer new styles of life to adults and adolescents alike. All of this making it possible, precisely, to imagine, constitute and organize the set of contemporary social tools, transformed into the harmonious expression of a machine-age civilization endowed at last, after a century of gestation, with the types of equipment which suit its own nature and, after a somber interval, restoring man to his position of supremacy and dignity.

It is thanks to the technical revolution which has been carried out that the architectural rebirth of the present day is beginning and will soon be mature enough to lead to *a homogeneous statute of building.*

But it is worth indicating three essential causes of this major transformation. *Since architecture is the visible sign of the spirit of an age,* there is nothing surprising about the fact that those causes proceed partly from the spiritual. Here they are:

a) the way in which the strength of materials is computed

b) an evolution of awareness

c) the aesthetic renewal accomplished in the plastic arts during the first cycle of the machine age.

a) The nineteenth century: the iron age—from the Pont des Arts in Paris to the Eiffel Tower, by way of the Crystal Palace in London, the halls where the Expositions Universelles were held in Paris—was like a lighthouse beam sweeping over the future. In addition to these great, ephemeral landmarks, achievements were marked in durable edifices: Labrouste's Bibliothèque Nationale, the steel department stores in Paris with or without iron and glass façades—the (old) Bon Marché, the Printemps, the Samaritaine. In Chicago, United States of America, Sullivan's first big buildings. At the same time, bridges of astounding boldness, such as Eiffel's Garabit, the George Washington Bridge in New York and the Golden Gate in San Francisco, etc. . . .

Such a break with the customs and traditions of building or aesthetics was to bring about an academic reaction. The sensational "intellectuals'" manifesto in Paris, demanding a halt to the erection of the Eiffel Tower, was one example. Later, after 1900, came a series of demolitions, erasing the Palais de l'Industrie, the Galérie des Machines, etc.

No matter what claims or protests are made today or were made yesterday, the architecture of iron and glass is a genuine revelation of the possibilities of our times. Reinforced concrete was born in France and developed there empirically at first but, towards 1900, this new technique became an exact science and the debate was open on aesthetic grounds. Violent reactions; some thought it cleverer to impose the traditional forms upon reinforced concrete. But men like Baudot, Tony Garnier and Auguste Perret especially, gave reinforced concrete its definitive place in architecture. Auguste Perret's colleagues at that time went so far as to challenge his right to the title of architect. . . . In forty years, reinforced concrete became the new building technique used throughout the world for the most daring projects: bridges, factories and dams, as well as for the most traditional ones: palaces or houses. . . . It took its place in domestic architecture to serve individual houses and, especially, big buildings.

Housing architecture adopted steel as well, not only for big buildings but also for the industrial mass production of the pre-fabricated individual house.

All over the world, architects are taking note of, reporting on these processes. . . . And it is France—France, the cradle of these daring techniques, that hesitates now to take advantage of the freedom which has been gained through so many new and precious resources.

At the same time, the building techniques used for railway tracks and cars, steamships or other ships, automobiles and airplanes are developing with unimaginable speed—marvelous yield of a joint effort by all the inventors the world over gathered around the same task. Architecture is an integral part of these programs. It is inserted into them, revealed in them, and in turn suddenly reveals dazzling horizons (efficiency and suitability). Architecture places its stamp on a throng of new things, bourgeons like spring, and radiates throughout the world. While a large share of its inventors are French, it is chiefly abroad that their effort is esteemed.

b) Starting in the second half of the nineteenth century, the misdeeds of the first machine age led to questioning as to where to situate the just, equitable point of view from which to envisage a favorable state of balance between man and machine. Now that industry had genuinely been brought into the world, now that the machines had become masters, men were dragged down into poverty and relentlessly pushed into an unnatural life. . . . Whereas, amidst the tumult of the industrial conquest, the machines were taken care of and pampered like goddesses, men were abandoned, left to drift where they would.

Century of steam, century of coal; therefore, black century. The countryside was covered with factories and dwellings. Housing was put up feverishly, negligently. The human condition was degraded to such a degree that the first warning symptoms of future revolutions appeared everywhere; prophets, some more valid than others, proclaimed the great, fundamental reforms which alone would be capable of giving a machine-born civilization the gift of harmony.

The question of aesthetics itself was raised.

Toward 1900 came the architectural schism which gave birth to the "nouveau style," the "modern style."

As early as 1850, Ruskin's preaching, on a genuinely lofty level, had called for a new state of consciousness to take responsibility for the destiny of the machine-age civilization. The arts spoke up, especially the one so closely attached to the human person: architecture. The puerile, costly and demoralizing pomp of official architecture was abandoned, and the dwelling of the new machine-age man, the humble and the rich, was given careful study. And within the dwelling, attention was given to the objects which are men's companions in life. This was a new viewpoint. To shake off the burden of artifice bequeathed by the centuries, men plunged into the examination and discovery of nature. A generation devoted itself to this study. But inevitably the problem had to be raised on its real merits which were not aesthetic but economic and social: how the ground should be occupied and, where buildings were concerned, their reasons for being or not being. City planning was to re-emerge out of a disastrous oversight, eternal discipline attached to the very life of societies. From then on, city planning and architecture, two interdependent things, were going to reconstitute the three-dimensional science which would place men *in the most favorable living conditions, in terms of both physical comfort and sensitivity.*

In 1943 it became clear that a question of consciousness was being raised throughout the universe . . . none other than the question of perceiving and picking out, from amidst all the confusion, the *reason for living.*

   c) *Technique and consciousness are the two levers of architecture on which the art of building rests.*

While on the one hand, architecture of any kind has to do with the strength of the materials it uses, on the other, it is inescapably dependent upon a phenomenon of a visual type: the plastic art.

Knowing, accurate and magnificent interplay of shapes assembled in the light.

In the course of the nineteenth and twentieth centuries, the plastic arts (painting and sculpture) revised their modes of expression, which had degenerated generally. Three generations were involved: *impressionism, fauvism* and *cubism*, in that order. (We might note in passing that their adversaries gave these efforts those labels, intended as so many insults.)

It was not until after the First World War that the architectural generation, armed with its new techniques, really came into contact with the plastic inventions.

Then it was that reinforced concrete, iron and glass found the basis for their aesthetic.

Had it not been for the last war, architectural experimentation would have been carried out on a universal scale. Specific features, born of climate or custom, would have emerged, piercing the very unity of this reinvigorated art, expression of a society carrying primeval common elements in its depths.

We are living right in the heart of the event, and as a result, we do not see it clearly. We do not measure it. You have to have traveled a great deal and compared a great deal in order to be able to realize the meaning of the present development, its intensity, its resources, its immediate probabilities, its unanimity.

In an attempt to belittle it, the adversaries of the new architecture have termed it "international" . . . and so they are acknowledging that unanimity has been achieved among builders and among users in all countries, at every latitude on this globe. This is precisely what the new architecture is accused of, a pejorative slant being put on the term "international." This flatters the reactionary spirit and the fear which have gripped the weak at heart when faced with the extravagances of this mutational period. S. Giedion stated, in his great history of architecture, *Space, Time, Architecture and City Planning*, that today, for the first time since the Baroque era, architecture possesses a style, but a style that is wide-meshed enough to give each region or country the opportunity of speaking its own language, if it is capable of doing so.

Thus, a contemporary style does exist. What are its characteristics? The change in viewpoint which modern society is experiencing originates in the technical inventions: computations of materials' strength, and the use of steel and reinforced concrete. Steel—the answer to problems of strength and the requirements of thrift, by means of the iron sections which heavy industry began producing in the nineteenth century and which are used either by themselves or together with reinforced concrete —the most subtle and accurate, as well as the most economical, of the recent techniques. This technique applies the contrasting characteristics of heterogeneous substances (steel and concrete) to the contrasting tensions, traction and compression, of one and the same piece.

Two events, separated by time at first, and brought together today. Steel, taking up the whole nineteenth century, being used to build bridges and huge, surprisingly shaped exhibition halls (besides, were the halls we have already mentioned anything other than bridges thrown over huge reaches of space—the Crystal Palace in London, the Palais de l'Industrie, the Galérie des Machines in Paris?). Reinforced concrete, which was not actually introduced until 1900, competing at first with steel in the construction of large ships or bridges, gradually took over the human dwelling and began to be used in putting up large buildings. In recent times the two processes seem to have been brought closer together to offer an economical solution to the problems of housing: reinforced concrete establishes the contact with the ground, as a valid foundation, and reaches the mezzanine platform from which the superstructure of the stories rises —the light and hollow cage where steel is perfect in its role.

Since offices (administrative headquarters of public or private firms) are intended, like the dwelling, to be the scene of sedentary occupations, they require the same type of volumes.

Both steel and reinforced concrete are particularly well suited for the building of *skeletons* of extreme, hitherto unknown, unforeseen lightness. Suddenly, the builder's ambition of providing light finds its undreamed of, total realization since the whole façade can become one glass wall (100% glass panes). Centuries had attempted this, in vain.[1] This was a technical revolution breaking with the accepted practice of builders and adepts of the plastic arts, and was quite capable of upsetting the aestheticians.

At the acme of his architectural glory, Louis XIV had no more adequate way of demonstrating his splendor, in the Hall of Mirrors at Versailles, than by using mirrors of mediocre dimensions. Today, mirrors are triumphant the world over, flawlessly smooth and transparent slabs whose dimensions are limited only by one accidental factor: the gauge of railway tunnels and bridges over roads.

1) Independent skeleton of steel or reinforced concrete: the first feature of today's style will be *lightness*.

2) Use of the transparent or translucent glass wall. The characteristic features will be: *light and limpidity*—Crystal Palace in London, or little houses surrounded by greenery and apartment or office buildings, in the most immediate future.

[1] Aside from the cathedrals, but the solution made the great height of the naves necessary; aside, too, from the Gothic style half-timbered private houses, whose Renaissance successors were the "grand' places" of Antwerp, Brussels, etc.

3) Accurate computation of the strength of steel and reinforced concrete shows how *economical* they are, in the highest sense of the word.

4) The new floorplans ensure good circulation, sound distribution, classification and orderliness, making the edifice as a whole a veritable exercise in biology (carrying skeleton, airy, light-filled space, cables and pipes supplying abundant "utilities" (water, gas, electricity, telephone, elimination of wastes, heating, ventilation, etc.). A feeling of *efficiency*.

5) The symphonic, harmonious and functional presence of so many new conditions introduced into the constructed work give it an undeniable character of conciseness and *accuracy*.

6) Straightness stems from the means used. The right angle is dominant. The needs to be satisfied: to create, for purposes of living in them and working in them, rooms or square premises. The technique of reinforced concrete answers these needs spontaneously (posts and struts, beams and girders, flat arches, rough-cast parts, etc. . . .). Ever since gusset plates ceased to be used for the setting of the post and the beams, as they were in the early days of reinforced concrete, the orthogonal position of the reinforced concrete wall has become obvious, *in the purity of its rectilinear form*.

7) Visual habits are renovated. The thick stone foundations which used to be necessary have been abandoned to a radical degree. The strong stone or masonry pillars, the walls whose thickness was dictated by their carrying functions—all of these prime factors in the feeling of plastic beauty, these detectors of a specific emotional quality are outclassed today by slim and sparingly used concrete or iron posts. When they first appeared, it was thought that they would never give the impression of being able to hold up a building, would never reassure the spectator sufficiently. . . . The years went by; we grew accustomed to the sight and aware of its elegance, the essential element of style today.

8) The roof-terrace, with drainpipes inside, is the normal, impermeable and completely safe type of roof, especially if it is planted with a garden which will protect the concrete and its iron elements from the very dangerous effects of expansion.

Flat roof and garden-terrace, drainpipes inside—this is one of the innovations which most profoundly upsets traditional aesthetics: An event of a technical nature, and consequently of universal value, which imposes itself everywhere, like the Gothic pointed arch, that knew no frontiers during the Middle Ages.

But a still more disturbing reform affects our acquired reflexes: the cornice, so useful and vivid for so long, the ostentatious corollary of the sloping roof, has fallen into disuse, since the water accumulating on the terrace is to be drained from the inside now, and no longer from the outside. As for protecting the façade, possibly a glass wall, there will be a new element to take care of that: the sunbreaker which, at the same time, will also be a rainshield. A device which constitutes a very appreciable additional convenience for the person using the premises.

9) From that point on, the materials traditionally used can be distributed in a new way.

Whereas, in the case of the small individual house, which will be erected by local craftsmen, customs and therefore the traditional attitude may persist, matters will be quite different where volumes of any real size are to be built.

Hewn stone will not set out to conquer the heights—an aimless conquest in this case. As man's eternal friend, it will remain in genuine contact with him, where he can touch it, in any of the countless pieces of constructed equipment which the reorganization of cities—and therefore, city planning—are bent on introducing. Wood will come down out of the rafters to panel the walls of mass-produced buildings, making them comfortable with a comfort that used to be reserved for the rich and powerful. And finally, the perishable metals will give way before the rustproof ones—steel, aluminum, etc. . . .

Such is the revolutionized architecture which is ready to serve city planning today. The type of programs which it has mapped out means that city planning will have considerable effect on the volume, arrangement and distribution of the various edifices which, in fact, constitute the efficient equipment of cities or rural communities.

The conquests of city planning will give a "new look" to apartment buildings, complete with their extensions, to business centers, or to certain places of work. Vertical, mechanical devices for circulation, flawless from the technical standpoint provided there is adequate organization, will make it possible for buildings to be put to perfect use—thus releasing a set of consequences the most important of which will be the mutual independence between constructed volumes and paths of circulation. In fact, the achievement of an exploit which, until now, had been thought chimerical: *the separation of pedestrians from automobiles*. Whereupon the constructed volume ceases to be the mere residue of the intersection of three or four streets; and the street itself ceases to be a corridor between the façades lined up all along both sides of it, while within those sides the most disparate things—pedestrians, horses, cars, trucks and trams—rush by amidst the most exasperating types of constraint. Reform which will yield magnificent fruit: a new career for each building, mistress of the surrounding free spaces, a magnificently architectural career for residential or work districts. Putting his technical conquest to use, man disposes of a style of the times which allows him at last to work toward his own well-being and aesthetic jubilation.

Atlas of the ways in which new ideas in architecture and city planning have been applied

In about 1900, in Tony Garnier's work called *La Cité Industrielle*, illustrated by a masterly series of drawings, something was proposed for the first time: the ground level of the city becomes public domain and lends itself to the installation of community equipment of value to all the inhabitants.

After a long eclipse, dignity and purity are once again, thanks to him, made an integral part of dwellings, places of work and of civic contact.

A few years later, Auguste Perret carried out his first reinforced concrete buildings, announcing a new aesthetic (Ponthieu garage, building in the rue Franklin, . . . Gobelins warehouse, etc. . . .).

After the First World War came the publication of *L'Esprit Nouveau*, an international review of contemporary activity which laid very special stress on the problems of architecture and city planning and aroused an interest in them which immediately spread beyond national borders. These ideas (ethical and aesthetic, technical and sociological) found expression (at the Salon d'Automne in 1922) in Le Corbusier's study entitled *A Contemporary City of Three Million Inhabitants*. The questions it raised about the dwelling (the cell for living, the rational site, including the future "statute of land for building" and the determination of "housing units of suitable size") were to become burning issues, what with city planning today taking all sorts of conditions—living, working, leisure and traffic—into account. In 1930, this tirelessly proposed, all-encompassing theme, architecture plus city planning, led to the definition of the idea known as the Radiant City.

The CIAM, or Congresses for Modern Architecture, had been founded in 1928, and for thirteen years they had devoted their efforts to city planning.

In 1933, the CIAM closed their Fourth Congress, in Athens, with a statement of "Findings" which were published ten years later as *The Athens Charter*.[2]

From year to year, city-planning themes and architectural solutions joined forces to answer the major questions which the times themselves were asking builders.

These efforts, surging out of every corner of the globe, were directly or indirectly linked to essential manifestations of the spiritual trend. In England, for instance, Ruskin's crusade and the appearance of garden cities; the city-planning theories of Camillo Sitte; the 1900 movement in art (Gaudi in Barcelona, Otto Wagner and Hoffmann in Vienna, Berlage in Amsterdam, Van de Velde in Brussels, Paris and Weimar, de Baudot and Guimard in Paris, Sant'Elia in Italy, Carl Moser in Zurich, Sullivan the precursor, then Wright in Chicago, and so on . . .); the irresistible advance of reinforced concrete, the building of cars, planes and steamships, the appearance of the first skyscrapers in the USA.

Today, some of these ideas, even though they have come from the remotest horizons, resemble some of the prophetic proposals that Fourier made in about 1830, just as the machine age was being born.

Moreover, certain features of plans for industrial cities fall in with the old Spanish idea of the "linear residential city" which goes back to 1880, but they are put to other purposes; and deep in the silence of the USSR, the idea was borrowed for certain projects included in the Five Year Plan.

Depending on various influences, depending on the local possibilities, a unanimous and universal impulse led to significant applications in every part of the world: Walter Gropius' proposals, reacting against the artificial, conformist character of what followed the first architectural awakening

2 Dazzling proof of this are the works published in New York, in Rio de Janeiro and in London but which did not reach Paris until 1945. They announce that by virtue of its government-commissioned building achievements, Brazil had taken the lead in modern architecture, having solved the problem of sunlight once and for all (and it was the first time that problem had been solved) in harmony with the demands of modern life in the tropics. Now, it happens that the basic elements of that renaissance had come from Paris.

in Germany; the Scandinavians' "Jugend Styl" (Stockholm—buildings with a social function, housing cooperatives, etc.); in Holland, the most recent city-planning projects for Amsterdam and an overall architectural renovation (houses, Van Nelle plant, offices, contest for plans for the Amsterdam Town Hall, etc. . . .). In Antwerp, in 1933, more than one half of the projects submitted to the international competition for the city-planning project concerning the left bank of the river Scheldt were of the "Radiant City" type. In Czechoslovakia, a strong movement in Prague, Brno, and Zlin (Batà). In the USSR, a strictly native movement called "constructivism" began to be supplemented, in 1928, by contributions from the West (International Competition for the Centrosoyus Palace and another for the Palace of the Soviets). In Switzerland, a number of applications throughout the country, and most especially in Zurich, Bern, Geneva, Basel. In Italy, the CIAM's very fruitful efforts in Milan. In Johannesburg (the Transvaal), the entire faculty of architecture at the university was won over to the CIAM's doctrine. London rallied to it in about 1932 (buildings, exhibits, city-planning projects for London itself). In Mexico City, a number of buildings. In Rio de Janeiro, a very active CIAM group builds the Ministry of Education and Public Health and draws up the plans for the University Center and many public buildings. Same activity in Uruguay and Argentina. And in the USA: Howe and Lescaze's distinctive skyscraper in Philadelphia; in New York, the Museum of Modern Art includes in its collections the scale models made in Paris for the Palace of the Soviets and for the development of Nemours in Algeria. Harvard University entrusts its chair of architecture to a member of the CIAM. In Algeria, the ceaseless effort to persuade the authorities to adopt a development plan consonant with the CIAM doctrine for Algiers and the surrounding region. The same sap rises in Hungary, Turkey, Poland, Yugoslavia, Greece. And China and Japan were among the first to put these ideas to enthusiastic use.

Not one country has remained unaffected by the revival. This architecture, this city planning that have spread throughout the world, having been born of computation (which is universal) and of a new awareness that emerged during the first cycle of the machine age, have features in common. All it will take is a few years of blossoming time, and local characteristics, imposed by climate and by custom, will become quite naturally visible in them.[3]

[3] The analysis of the new residential conditions was embodied in the 3rd section of ASCORAL: Sub-section on household equipment.

CHAPTER 4
The rules: human beings and nature

There will be rules to this mutation. Part of them will be the bouquet of ideas and inventions making up the building facts which belong to the first cycle, first century of the machine age. Others have been arrived at by induction and reasoning, in line with that process by which the mind recognizes and denounces the present chaos and formulates proposals which express, successively, acquired certainties and unanimous aims. In order to draw up these rules, *readers of the situation*, explorers of the near tomorrow, are needed. And the only people who can be accepted as readers are those who are capable of offering something with which to replace whatever their criticisms demolish. They are not abstractors of the quintessential but builders. They have not escaped into abstract notions; they have not put on vague masks rather than step straight into the arena and struggle with all the difficulties; generalizations are not their goal. *Generalizations* are used to confirm the idea that new notions have the right to live. It is not that generalizations will lead one day to the invention or the discovery of new notions; things work the other way around. Life is made of spontaneous inventions, and those which can be or are confirmed by generalization bring life and harmony with them. The others: so much failure, hiatus.

Those who bring a rule must be *inventors*, and not *deducers*.

Where building is concerned, and that is what concerns us here, what are those axioms that have been hawked from century to century and have choked to death by now—the three orders of architecture, the styles, the rules dictated by da Vignola? They are the remains of bygone civilizations; kept alive despite all reason, they are nothing more today than false witnesses. In order to evaluate the answers to the imposing questions raised by our times about the ways of equipping it, the one acceptable unit of measurement, which will reduce every question to its basic elements, is *the human being*.

These creatures, these human beings, this society of today are plunged into their environment. Any attempt to dodge the issue would be chimerical and quickly punished.

So an equilibrium must be sought between man and his environment.

But what environment, what man is concerned here? A man profoundly altered by the artifice of centuries of civilization and, in this instance, especially a man frightfully exasperated by a hundred years of the machine age? An environment of frenzy, the tumult of mechanical things, a sometimes hallucinating spectacle and atmosphere?

Neither one. In these troubled times, we go back directly to the very principles which constitute the human being and his environment. Man considered as a biological phenomenon—psycho physiological value; the environment, its permanent essence, explored anew—and turning out to be nature. . . . Find the law of nature once again. And contemplate man and his environment—fundamental man and profoundest nature.

Seek, find, rediscover the unity which presides over human efforts and those of nature. Man, a product (perhaps the supreme product) of Nature and therefore mirror of Nature; Nature, part of the cosmos. So that harmony may reign, the very spirit which inhabits nature must be injected into the undertakings of the spirit.

The human effort must be made to support, second the work of nature. Nature provides us with an unlimited quantity of lessons. Life is manifest in them; biology gathers all their rules together. In the lessons of nature, everything is birth, growth, bloom, decline. The conduct of men also proceeds from analogous movements. Architecture and city planning, by means of which men give their own life its appropriate setting, are the most accurate expression of a society's material and moral values. Here again, life determines ideas: birth, development, blooming, decline. Biology is a term eminently suited to architecture and city planning: biology, the qualities of living architecture, vivid city planning. Biology overseeing the plans and cross sections of the buildings, coordinating the volumes, responding to functional needs, making for flexible and harmonious circulation. Life develops outward from within and blossoms, open to light, offered to space. Architecture and city planning proceed from that unifying rule — outward from within — which passes severe judgment on all about it. And so we have the act of building, using elements which are brought together for specific purposes and which are so many organs, coherent as the organs in natural organisms.

The unity which is in nature and in man is the law which brings the created thing to life. Once the rule has been acknowledged and accepted, the parasites, the residues are stripped of their rights. Renewal is what lies at the heart of natural events, whether seasonal events within each solar year or cyclical events, such as civilizations. Our societies too have experienced incessant renewal. If you know how to climb up high enough, stand back far enough from the circumstances of day-to-day, then you can make out the cycles or the seasons; you can read them. And the spontaneous inventions, or those occurring in strings of related con-sequences, have shot up so vigorously that, having dethroned the pre-machine-age civilization (painful though we find this and cling as we may to the dethroned present), they have installed a new point of view and the adjustments which will be made accordingly will be like a keen set of tools placed in the hands of the individual and the group.

May the word "tool" shed the light of its fullest meaning on the effort for efficiency which is expected of the newly constituted organs of our society.

CHAPTER 5

Acquiring a set of tools

Tools are the useful extensions of a man's arms and legs. This definition can be stretched to cover certain products of human ingenuity which are also intended to second the person as such: the dwelling is a tool, and so are the road, the workshop, and so on.

The tools are to be used to perform functions. E. T. Gillard lines them up along three main axes, each based on one of the three fundamental stages in the evolution of organized beings: the stomach, the genitals and the head — three organs responsible for nourishment, reproduction and thoughts. When transposed to the social level, they become economic, patriarchal and spiritual values, which in turn form the matrices of the key (economic, patriarchal and spiritual) institutions.

The point of introducing this dialectic here is to lead us, or bring us back, to the only question capable of dominating the discussion: the question of forging tools corresponding to the life functions (living, dwelling, working, cultivating the body and the mind) to which a lofty but attainable goal may be assigned: *the joy of living*. Which does not mean that the plans will not be dictated by the most thoroughgoing objectivity.

The tools of city planning will take the form of architectural *units*, animated in each case by the rigorous principles of biology which alone is capable of assuming these tasks. A unit of time will measure the way in which space is distributed: the solar unit of the twenty-four-hour day which establishes the rhythm of our undertakings and our acts.

A sound and healthy body, an environment favorable to reproduction, persistent joy of living despite the disappointments and accidents of fate, each of those goals can be broken down into a quantity of others, each of them calling upon architecture and city planning for *sites and premises, specific and effective objects, indispensable tools*. These are the essential, constituent facts of the-thing-which-is-built and, similar to living beings in their unity, their integrity, their harmony, they can be overseen perfectly.

The newspaper columnists, those "troubadours" who periodically chant the poetry of the old cities and the old countryside, closing their eyes to the tragedy of the untouchables in their rotting hovels and sagging farms, will excite public opinion against the tools and equipment we are proposing here in order to introduce the joy of living into the destiny of countries, cities and villages. They will rhapsodize about scents while we will be busy, here, drawing up a descriptive inventory of equipment that will endow the whole country with objects conceived with the accuracy and vigor of the principles and rules without which no blueprint can be drawn or brought to the actual building stage. Tools are made of substances, arranged in certain ways, and not of words and fancy phrases. Tools perform functions, and functions make up daily life. Wouldn't it be lovely — but chimerical, alas — if we could hear those troubadours happily singing their discovery of the joy of living right in the midst of this machine-age society finally installed in a suitable setting, equipped at last with what it really needs, acting at all times with the freedom of a bird in the sky?

For poetry can be read into the purpose which has determined the shape of things.

By way of preamble to proposals for the present, we might take a look at the old set of tools used by architecture and city planning. That way, we will see that things have their *reasons for being*. And once those reasons no longer exist, then reason or common sense says that the burden of their uselessness should not clutter up our lives.

1. Reason can be conceptual or corrective. Corrective when the purpose is to make an orderly arrangement out of a series of events having occurred independently of one another — the sort of adventure that has taken place around the cradle of so many cities; conceptual when the mind was master of the action, put to the task of guaranteeing men, through the planning of their cities, the most favorable living conditions — an event which is proper to certain civilizations, certain hours of

history, certain favorable and fortuitous encounters.

Here are a few of the forms taken by a preconceived type of city planning, cradle of cities: the Roman enclosures in Gaul. In French this is called *une enceinte*, and *enceinte* means both *that which encloses* and the *pregnant* woman who carries an infant in her womb. From these images we take the principle of a form deliberately shaped with the intention of being the vessel containing a city. Within it, a circulation network feeds the soil protected by the walls. Gates are opened in the enclosing walls from which roads lead away into the countryside.

This is how the Romans prepared a city, without hesitating to submit to the strict demands and unforeseeable dangers of a forecast. The reward for their wisdom was, not unforeseeables, but certainties, positive elements of city planning, means by which to create favorable conditions all around the inhabitants.

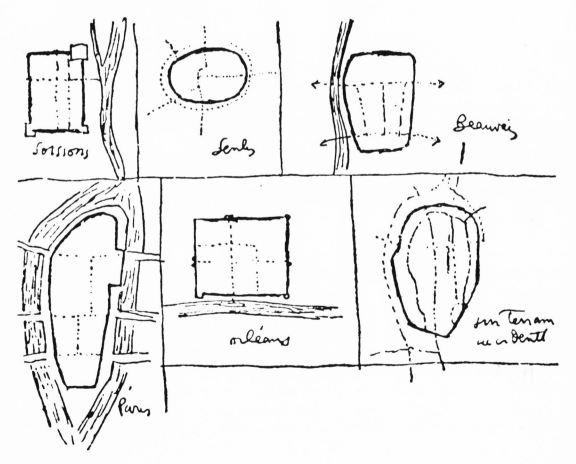

Let's remember this principle of the anticipated view, the preconceived form, a common measure, as it were, between the human rules and the natural features of the terrain. Let's remember the decision to proceed by stages, with the risks but also the advantages that that involves.

2. Additional equipment: having built walls all around the cities, the Romans then erect towers to defend those walls.

Then, for their water supply, they launch aqueducts from far away across the countryside.

Walls, towers and aqueducts may make noble architectural visions and, later on, touching ruins. But that is merely a consequence, a possible transfer of a utilitarian intention to a higher level of plastic or lyrical effect.

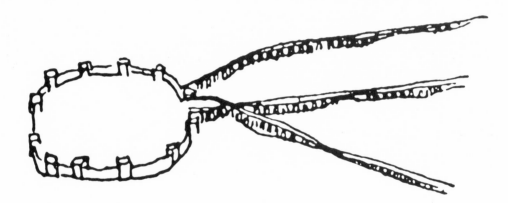

3. The Roman camp at Rouen became the medieval city: the enclosing walls, the roadways and public squares remained. The cathedral rises where once stood the basilica of Roman justice, etc. *Fuori-muro*, the bridge and the road to the south, the gates at the cardinal points — throughout the ups and downs of the city, all of these bear witness to the Roman will . . .

Then the second stage begins. This one is not inspired by a conceptual spirit shaped by the great experience acquired gradually over the thousands of years of those civilizations whose grandeur and magnificence illuminated the rim of the Mediterranean.

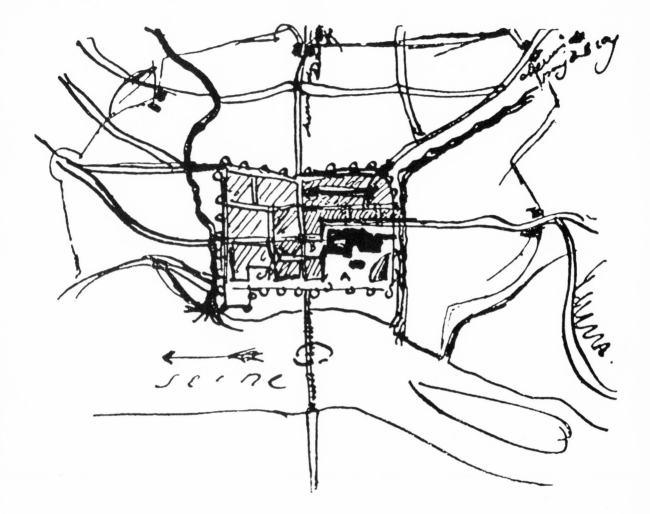

Instead it is left to chance, to the improvisation of a society made of new and still barbarian sedimentary deposits. Outside the walls, the edges of the narrow lanes or main roads were rapidly hugged by houses, so that routes which should have been only rural, not urban were petrified and, as the years went by, they weighed heavier and heavier on the city's growth. The ultimate and immeasurable result was to prevent any orthogonal lay-out and, instead, to make the curving, oblique or twisting street unavoid-able, laying a vise-like grip on the centuries to come, down to the present day. Things had been allowed to go their own sweet way, and no more effort was made to forge tools for the work or the life of the city.

35

4. Medieval equipment: the waters (the Seine) as rampart; the choice of an island as base. A fortified, crenellated turreted wall. Where the gate opens, a small fortress stands to defend the drawbridge — for the stone bridge over the Seine stops short of the river bank. On the island, another small defensive fortress. At the end of the second bridge, still another small fortress, then two arches of the bridge, finally another fortress. The last section of the bridge is made of wood, so that it can be burned quickly before the assailant.

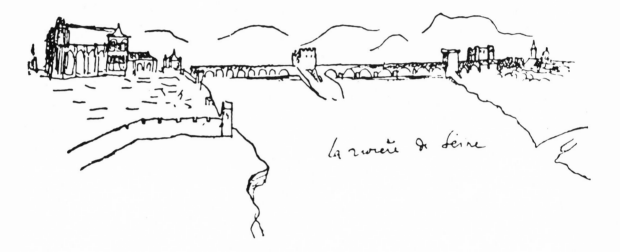

It is beyond this perfect and minutely detailed military defense installation that the false town (*le faux bourg*) begins — sacrificed, of course.

In the town, the well-protected cathedral rises, lofty, tool of prayers.

5. Antwerp in the seventeenth century: its vital organs are as clear and differentiated as the hammer, the pliers and the chisel in a toolbox.

a) A circulatory system which is the lifeblood of the city: the Scheldt, where cargoes from the Indies and the Americas arrive; three roads, which lead to France, to Burgundy, to Germany. Antwerp on the mouth of the river Scheldt, a trading city whose destiny was written into its geography.

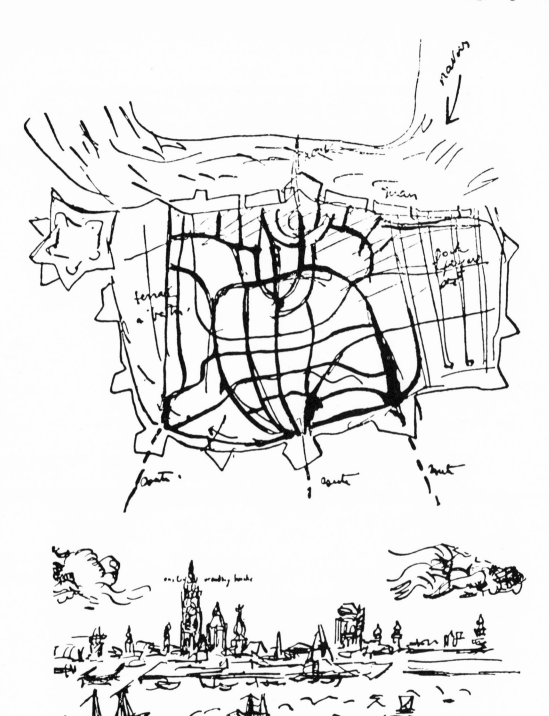

All along the river, loading and unloading installations; on the city's eastern flank, the docks, with their warehouses and their complement of roads and canals divided into regular compartments. In the center, a residential city with its merchants' mansions and the dwellings of workers and craftsmen, its churches and its cathedral, its town and guildhall, the *business center*. To the west, more land for building on, kept in reserve. And then the defense works, the strongbox and its locks: first of all, the fortress on the left banks of the river Scheldt, facing the docks and covering them with its cannon; secondly, westward, another fortress against an inland enemy; thirdly, everywhere else, fortified walls that enclose the city, its docks and its future building sites.

There is no denying that this city had the city fathers it needed, when it needed them!

6. Whereas the Greek city expressed itself, in the straightness of right angles, through its stadia, its agora, its market place, its palaestrae, and its temples, the Western city, on the contrary, was the theater of struggles for violent century after violent century, internal struggles even, and its outlook reflected all this violence. All it built was walls, battlements, fortresses and towers. The tools of a wild animal; splendor like that of a tiger.

7. The same tiger families imported a Byzantine theme, the loggia, as a leisure-time place, for playing chess or cards, for making music and dancing, for feasting and nuptial celebration. Equipment for grace and worldliness.

8. Equipment for the sacred life: the conspicuous cathedral. Pure vessel devoted to fervor and enthusiasm. The nave is an extraordinary triumph of purity, the reward of a flawless building system, bringing mathematical equations together with metaphysics and esoterica. Here is the center of the people's life, bursting with joy and with the God the people have given themselves.

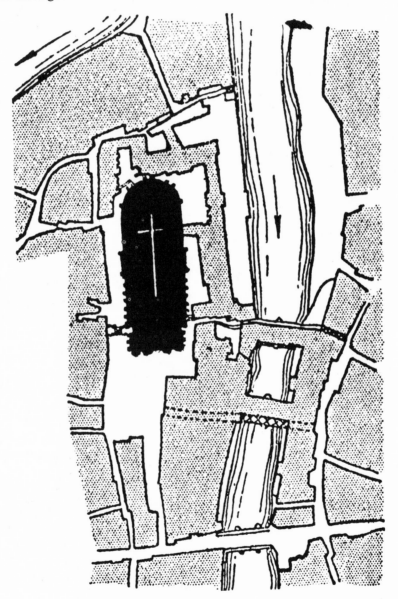

Sometimes the envelope, the stone epidermis covering the audacious skeleton is rough, shaggy: never mind. Anyhow, that doesn't bar the way for creative power or prevent the spirit from expressing itself freely. Here, Notre Dame in Paris; there, Notre Dame in Rouen, and so on . . .

Paris

Rouen

Grandeur of intention does not make light of material grandeur; height — man's constant aspiration — triumphs here and will carry its message down through all the centuries. Message of courage, boldness, temerity even. Which in fact is a beautiful message.

Tool of grandeur and splendor, pointing to a state of mind which was able to radiate over everything at one point.

Rouen

This rapid glance back into time has lingered mostly on a set of tools which was always renewed as the years went by: the military defense installation.

The type of defensive works was determined by the type of the offensive weapons. Era of walls later replaced by bastions, redoubts, and recessed *redents*. The city continued to be squeezed, almost choked — and this accounted for so many features which were contrary to men's well-being: narrow streets and courtyards.

Then came a day when offensive weapons made mock of military enclosures, when the advent of the airplane meant that fortresses no longer had ceilings — a recent event, since it dates from the First World War. From then on, military requirements were to take other forms, even, ironically enough, the opposite form, turning their back on the traditional features: aerial defense uses wide-open spaces, the principles of concentration in narrow but high-rising buildings and of doing away with courtyards — requirements which, miraculously, and by pure chance, went halfway to meet architectural and city-planning initiatives stemming from other causes and yet calling for similar arrangements. For the question involved was, and is, that of housing human beings.

The question is that of wresting a whole society from its hovels, looking for the well-being of men, achieving the material conditions which correspond naturally to their occupations. A set of tools to be forged through the form, volume and arrangement of perfectly efficient units, each intended to perform functions which take up, or should take up, the day-to-day allotment of time: housing units comprising the dwelling and the extensions of it; work units: workshops, factories and mills, offices; units for spiritual and physical education; agricultural units, of the only type capable of combining the material and spiritual factors of a peasant rebirth; and finally, linking all these things and bringing them to life, the circulation (or traffic) units — horizontal, for pedestrians and cars, and vertical.

Efficiency will be an aim, of course. But efficiency cannot be defined except in terms of an a priori . . . which is not, in this case, the glorification of technology but, on the contrary, putting technology to use to serve men. This point of view, coming after the squalls of the first cycle of the machine age, is the fruit of a new philosophy. For instance, today, at a time when many people are drunk on speed and both technicians and city fathers have lost their heads over it, walking will be considered as the first desirable goal, a priori, which should influence the way cities are laid out. At a time when aviation begins to reign over the inferno of war and could aspire to be the delight of our peacetime existence, the a priori will be the idea that aviation should be banned from the sky above any city, since a free and silent sky is a boon to all men. And so on.

This attitude means that efficient units are conceived in terms of their internal arrangement, in terms of a biological virtue, so to speak, and that efforts are made to calculate their useful size. The task at this point is to determine housing units of suitable size, fruits of the architectural revolution which has taken place and of reinvigoration through city planning. Creation of a set of tools made of units satisfying specific purposes. These units within the city will be as the town is within the nation: an operational basis, for a housing unit of suitable size runs itself perfectly well.

CHAPTER 6

CREATING A SET OF CITY-PLANNING TOOLS TO BE USED BY THE MACHINE AGE SOCIETY

HOUSING UNITS: THE DWELLING AND EXTENSIONS OF THE DWELLING

What we are talking about here is a set of tools, housing tools placed in the hands of living creatures and based on psycho physiological constants which have been duly recognized and inventoried by competent people (biologists, doctors, physicists and chemists, sociologists and poets). The purpose of these tools is to facilitate living conditions, ensure the moral and physical health of the inhabitants, foster the perpetuation of the species by providing the facilities which are necessary for a perfect education, introduce the joy of living and bring out and develop the social feelings which can lead to civic-mindedness—the attitude that generates the action which elevates the town as a whole to the utmost level of awareness and dignity.

The dwelling is a *containing vessel* corresponding to certain conditions and establishing valuable relationships between the cosmic surroundings and the human biological phenomena. In it a man (or a family) will live—sleeping, walking, hearing, seeing and thinking. Regardless of whether he is motionless or moving about, the premises he occupies must cover an adequate area and also be of a height suited to his gestures. The furniture or the features built into his dwelling are like an extension of his own limbs or functions. Biological necessities imposed by habits thousands of years old and which, little by little, have gone to make up his very nature, demand the presence of specific elements and conditions —sun, space, greenery—without which he is in danger of withering away.

For his lungs, air of an appropriate quality. For his ears, a sufficient quantum of silence. For his eyes, favorable light. Etc. . . .

Assuming that the dwelling has succeeded in providing this sort of conditions, that is still not enough. Man today, at the present stage of his behavior as a civilized being and of his social relationships, requires additional services which are provided by organizations that are external to his dwelling, services that have been termed, *extensions of the dwelling*. We say, *extensions of the dwelling*, so as to make it clear that these essential conveniences are a part of his daily life and therefore should be within easy reach. If they were unreasonably far out of his way, then hardship, fatigue and wear would set in; and these are not fleeting but daily evils, since they begin all over again every single day all one's life long. They are pitiless—as can clearly be seen in certain types of degeneracy or certain social crises. The crisis puts the blame on the tool that has become worthless because, worn out or ineffectual, it doesn't do its work any more. It should be thrown away, far away.

There are two types of extensions of dwelling. Strictly material services, first of all: food supply, cleaning and other household chores, hygiene, physical fitness and improvement. Then, extensions of more specifically spiritual scope: the infants' nursery, kindergarten, primary school, arts and crafts for young people.

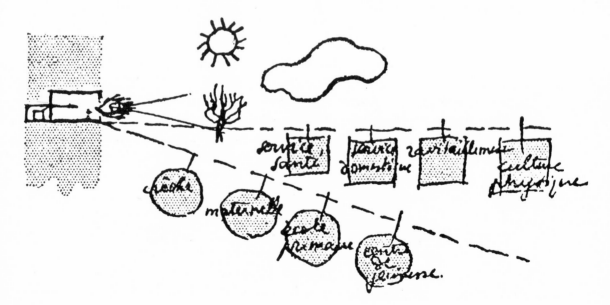

Depending on whether these tools for daily use are located nearby or far away, based on the amount of time needed to reach them within the twenty-four solar day, they make for pleasure or hindrance.

The dwelling can take two forms: the isolated individual house, or the large building where organized communal services are available. The first form would seem to guarantee its inhabitant freedom itself, while the second would seem to create a set of restraints all about him. But when both solutions are put into effect within the community, the results are seen to differ very widely from the ones they were hastily assumed to produce. That is because the time-distance function intervenes, reversing the situation once a certain population figure is reached or once the means of transportation offered within the network of circulation channels (streets) prove inadequate to a certain extent.

Only a wise appraisal of the various factors involved will lead to a timely choice of the solution which offers a "human" advantage.

Here are two types of individual houses that correspond to differing states of sensitivity; they are suited to thinly populated areas. On the other hand, it is indispensable to know that when the same forms are used

in carrying out garden cities within a large urban center, they cover such an enormous amount of surface that they denaturalize the urban phenomenon itself and lead to modern waste on a mammoth scale (waste in terms of means of transportation, utility mains and the user's time), swallowing up outrageous budgets and crushing modern society under that unexpected burden which is nothing other than a new type of slavery, since the only way to make up for the added expenditure is by assuming an added workload of as much as two, three or four hours every day.

This sickness is not peculiar to just one unfortunate and disfigured city; it has spread throughout the new world and the old; Paris and its suburbs, London, Berlin, Moscow, Rio de Janeiro, Buenos Aires, São Paolo, New York, Chicago, Algiers.

The very thing which is helping along a respect of the *time-distance* function, reinstating human living conditions (biology and cosmos), is the present trend in the building art. For population centers of any real size, the reform will lie in the erection of *vertical garden cities*, taking up where horizontal garden cities leave off.

Organization of the elements needed in order to run the dwelling and its extensions easily can be shown in the following sketch:

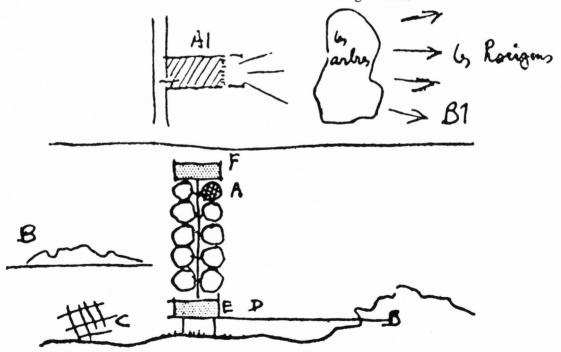

Dwellings A and A1 are placed in their natural setting: horizons, sunlight, greenery. The surroundings that the CIAM's Athens Charter called for as early as 1933—sun, space, greenery—are there, guaranteed by the measures the city fathers have taken. B and B1 indicate trees and horizons. The natural ground surface is given the best possible safeguard by the fact that the network of footpaths is separated from the network of roads for mechanized vehicles.

So it is that, despite the vertical arrangement of the cells-for-living-in, the advantages which the horizontal garden cities aim to provide are also provided here. But the *raison d'être* of these vertical garden cities lies in the organization of communal services.

C indicates huge available land surfaces, part of which will be devoted to the sports that are practiced daily (areas for walking, for ball games and for races, swimming pools, etc.). Another part will be set aside for individual kitchen gardens, which will be allotted upon request but which, because they are grouped, can be watered and irrigated virtually automatically. Natural variations in the topography will be taken advantage of for landscaping purposes. The footpaths will lead to specific destinations since the roadways for cars will be separate and independent. The latter network, serving the housing units, will be simplified to a considerable extent (highways either carried by viaducts or running through trenches or semi-trenches or tunnels).

A set of innovations will relieve each mother of what has been until now an overwhelming burden of household chores: there will be a food supply service (at E) in each housing unit as well as a service providing household help; at F, a *health unit* will be set up, consisting of physical culture gymnasiums, hydrotherapy and heliotherapy equipment, preventive medicine facilities with dispensary, small clinic for emergency cases, etc.

The organic and architectural arrangement of elements around the nucleus sketched on the facing page leads to a characteristic organization of constructed volumes. Making them a symmetrical composition in every direction all around a vertical axis is out of the question, since one of the factors essential to the dwelling—that is, the amount of sunshine—depends on a function which is not circular but frontal (the path the sun follows from its rising to its setting) and the height of which varies from the winter solstice to the summer solstice. The constructed volume

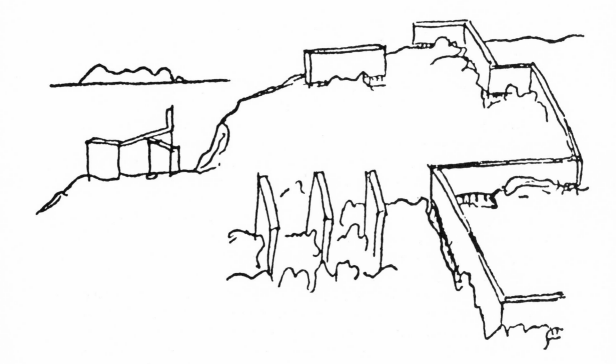

becomes the result of a combination of human biology and cosmic elements. Pure and flawlessly regulated attitude, but which makes allowance for extremely diversified types.

Those variations will be dictated by the nature of the site (topography and horizons), the way the district in question is oriented, the climate, etc.: Y-shaped (1), I-shaped (2), frontal (3) or indented (4) constructed volumes—as shown in the illustration on the facing page.

Above all else, it should be noted that these constructed volumes, conceived as veritable tools, contribute power, wealth, beauty and architectural splendor. And since they obey such rules as these, the residential zones will offer a vision of clarity, grace, orderliness and elegance.[4]

Work units

The processing of raw materials is done in workshops, mills and factories.

Administrative work, whether private or public, is done inside offices.

Trade, in shops or stores.

Farm work, on the ground, but at the same time it necessitates equipment for gathering and distributing produce, for storage and for the maintenance of machines.

Workshops, mills, factories, offices, shops and stores, farming facilities—all these constitute so many specific objects, accurate tools governed as much by the rules of human biology as by the rules of transportation and circulation.

These tools make it possible to do the work in the most rapid and careful way and to receive or ship raw materials or manufactured articles. They must measure up to indispensable sanitation requirements; but even more important, they must help to create joy in work. Work need not be inflicted, imposed like a punishment or the payment of a debt. Since work is the very key of existence, it would be preferable if work were looked on as something promising joy and if organization had the cooperation of good will and imagination so that work became a pleasing exercise, as it is already for certain handicraft vocations or professional callings—or perhaps it would be more accurate to say, as it is already for certain individuals, with certain types of character; having made

4 It is worth noting that when the elevator is left in the user's hands, it is limited to a speed of approximately 60 meters a minute; whereas when entrusted to a professional elevator operator, it can travel 300 meters a minute.

enough of a moral effort, they have seen the positive viewpoint take shape before them. There is an unmistakable feeling that an ethical system can be derived from a material and spiritual effort toward organization and that from then on, those ethics will place a different interpretation on the burdens or the joys of life.

CITY: WORKSHOPS, FACTORIES, MILLS

Lighted floor space; healthy air, elimination of dust, reliable receipt and dispatch of raw materials or manufactured articles. The workshop can be occupied by one person or by five or a hundred. It can be in a village or in a city and be used for handicrafts, maintenance and repair work or any especially creative activity. The workshop is part of the very life of the community or the city. Maintenance and repair work are linked to the residential areas (plumbers, locksmiths, carpenters, electricians, etc.). If the work involves creating imaginative products on a high level of craftsmanship, it will be located at the more intensive points of urban life (sewing, fashion, sheathing, bookbinding, leather work, goldsmithing, jewelry, clockmaking, foundries, wrought iron, etc.).

A factory or mill calls for the same sort of conditions but more extensively, on a very different scale. It can bring together an unlimited number of men or women workers. But the size of the building itself will necessarily obey a rule stemming from the conditions in which the work is controlled. When you come right down to it, the job of controlling (giving orders and seeing that they are carried out) is entrusted to a single individual: the foreman. The exact amount of area he is capable of overseeing will be determined by measurements of the distance his footsteps are to cover repeatedly every day and the distance his eyes can take in.

Whereupon units of area, varying from one industry to another, become clear.

Those units can be used to subdivide the overall area devoted to manufacturing installations within a huge complex of workshops. Or, in

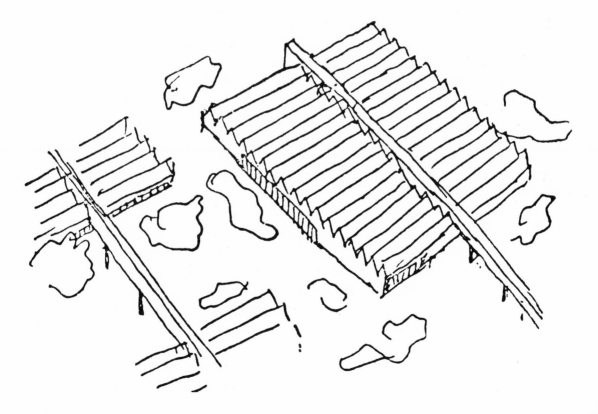

another form, they can determine how big each workshop should be within the manufacturing group as a whole.

Craftsmen's workshops in the cities or villages, factories and mills in the linear cities, both are the scene of jobs which, depending on the architecture and the city planning used, will be joyous, morose or discouraging—and both of them, provided due consideration has been given to respect for the human individual, can constitute new "green zones" of work, "green workshops," "green mills." Initiatives which are incumbent upon the authorities and transmitted to the city planner and the architect, bringing the landscaping element into the basic elements that go to make up a work unit.

An instinctive notion which has been somewhat run down, alas, amidst the disorder of the first cycle of the machine age, will re-emerge as a vital condition of work: that of keeping things clean and in good repair (the windows, once washed, will bring the friendly sight of lawns, trees and sky right into the workshop). This is no mere flight of fancy, since examples are already to be found in the United States, Switzerland, Germany, Czechoslovakia, Scandinavia, etc.

Since heavy industry calls for various types of premises, and it in turn, through architecture and city planning, can alleviate the harshest working conditions, we will have "green factories" in which machines will not be the only things held to be of any value and coddled and meticulously kept in good condition: men—the labor force—will be the focal point of imaginative efforts. Work can cease to be an act of contrition.

CITY: OFFICES, TRADE

Lighted floor space, healthy air, suitable silence, contacts facilitated, inauguration of a complex set of tools for the transmission of ideas and orders by telephone, telegraph, radio, mail, etc. . . . , the office is a place of work for one person, or five or a hundred or a thousand.

The office is naturally located in the heart of the urban circulatory systems. Since each office is the site of countless contacts, the offices should be close to one another. As a matter of fact they have already, in every city, been grouped into a single district, a very specific part of the city, "the business district." Better still, they tend to be grouped in a single building, a flawless office building: the business city. The business city means contacts and mutual independence, rapidity, time-saving. Where private or public administration is concerned, time takes on a very special significance; it is more precious, the minutes are more valuable. Efficiency must prevail so that orders and control can gather all things and people together effectively in the brief daily period—six or eight hours —of office work.

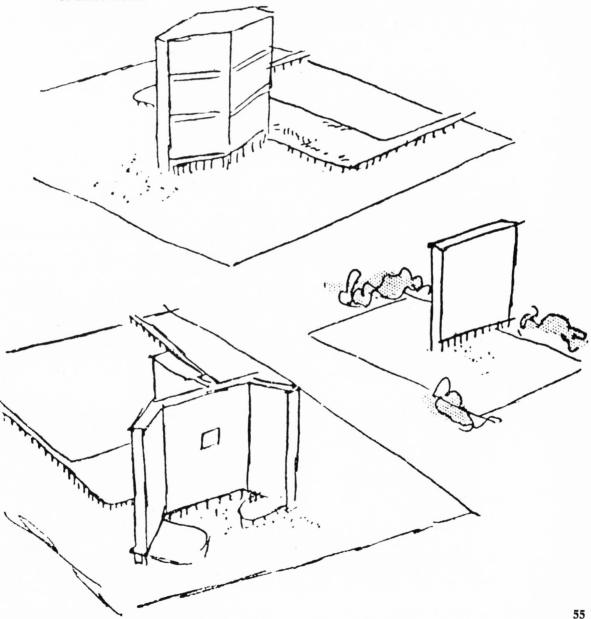

Depending on the size of the city, depending on the resources or obligations of the city-planning projects, depending too on a matter of *taste* which makes it very possible to choose among the various forms which are acceptable—depending on all these elements, businesses will be grouped in the business city, and the business city (district) will be made up of a certain limited or unlimited number of edifices specially planned and equipped for that purpose, *office units* which can often be reduced to a single building, constituting the *business city* within the city.

Two phenomena which are related in time but require the most rigorous separation in space will determine the biology of the business city: ground-level circulation (pedestrians and vehicles), and sedentary work in the offices.

The business city automatically has the heaviest population density of any place in town and, as a result, intense movement and flow at the very foot of its edifice or edifices. It is only natural therefore to set aside an appropriate traffic and parking area. Until now, business cities have developed where chance has let them—the chance of private initiatives, of the most virulent competition, of land that is available and unbespoke by any city-planning project. Hence the inextricable situation in which New York, Chicago or Buenos Aires finds itself, or, in another form, Algiers, Paris or London.

Like the dwelling, the office is linked, first of all, to a certain order of cosmic conditions; the law of the sun (orientation determining light, temperature and radiant energy). Next, it requires proper air (component elements and temperature); the most favorable lighting in every corner of the premises so that they can be put to optimum use; inside and outside contacts, the prerequisite being a shortening of distances (problem of horizontal circulation on each floor and vertical circulation by elevators, freight lifts, stairways, escalators, etc.); the form and surface area of the floors will in fact depend on the limits set by the necessity of rapid contact. And lastly, still one more necessity: that of being able to dispose of reliably lighted premises, whether small, medium-sized or large or grouped in useful combinations, as well as the possibility of expanding or reducing the area or the number of offices without bothering the neighbors and without endangering the sturdiness of the building.

We can safely say that never has any set of tools, any piece of equipment been more accurately defined by thoroughly well-known and current conditions than has today's business city.

Trade, on the other hand, is a matter of shops and stores.

The first, essential category of shops has already been classified in its proper place: food supply has become a function intimately linked to the dwelling.

There remain the other shops, more or less closely assimilated to one-man outlets, and also the veritable nuclei of modern trade: the department stores.

Several forms are possible, depending on the case:

The one-man outlet type of shop can be a significant unit in the urban pattern—the street of luxury or craftsmen's shops.

This type of production, which does not correspond to mass needs but, on the contrary, to personal tastes, requires very specially designed exhibit and display spaces frequented by an experienced public at those

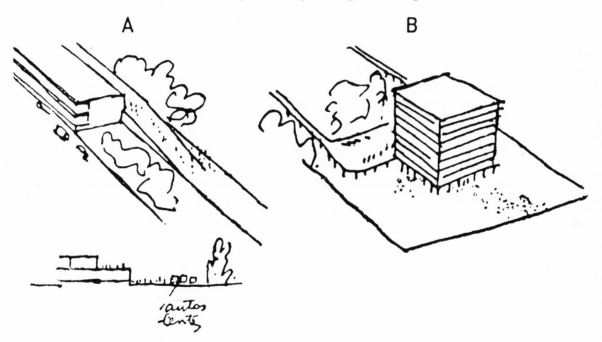

leisure hours when everyone feels like strolling and looking about. These units can take the most varied forms—the one shown in figure A is typical.

The department store is nothing other than a vast container, a huge storehouse; separate traffic systems for pedestrians and vehicles are arranged in front of it (B).

COUNTRY: RURAL CENTERS

Among the set of tools for gathering and distributing storage products and for the maintenance and repair of machines, we have the "silo" for grain, fruits, vegetables, tubers (the produce of the soil grouped in sufficient bulk, sorted and graded in regular qualities; the peasant protected from exploiters because he is guaranteed shelter for his harvests, allowing him to gain time). Both the combustion engine and electricity penetrate deeper and deeper into peasant life; machines appear and require suitable cover and the attention of specialized mechanics.

Once it has been introduced into peasant life, the new set of work instruments will necessitate special forms of rural centralization, coming under the heading of general readaptation of rural regions.

LEISURE TIME UNITS

Very different types of equipment, ranging from the smallest to the largest, from sports facilities for everyday use to the great center of public rejoicings, able to hold 100,000 people—Olympics, gymkhanas, open-air theater or grand pageants, processions, etc. Lastly, facilities for spiritual leisure (libraries, theaters and clubs, concert auditoriums and lecture halls, exhibition halls, etc., and youth centers, workshops or clubs specifically intended for adolescents).

In these infinitely varied things, architecture will be the master.

Cafés, restaurants, shops (discussed above) will be what remains of today's street (scene of bustling but disorganized activity) but they will be rearranged, put into orderly and fully effective shape. Places designed for strolling and sociability, for hubbub and a certain confusion conducive to fun.

Physical culture will be practiced, for the most part, on ground level —transformed into a park—in residential areas: athletics, ball games, swimming, walking, racing, etc. To some extent too, it will be in the very heart of the buildings themselves, in premises set aside for physical culture and for helio- and hydro-therapy. All of these facilities perfectly defined.

Traffic units

HORIZONTAL TYPES OF CIRCULATION

Their primary mission is to dispel the confusion between natural speeds (man's footsteps) and mechanized speeds (automobiles, buses, trams, bicycles and motorcycles) by making the appropriate distinctions.

The corollary will be to create parking areas outside of the traffic areas.

The word *street* nowadays means, chaotic circulation. Let us replace the word (and the thing itself) by the terms, *footpaths* and *automobile road* or *highway*. And let us organize each of these two new elements in relation to the other.

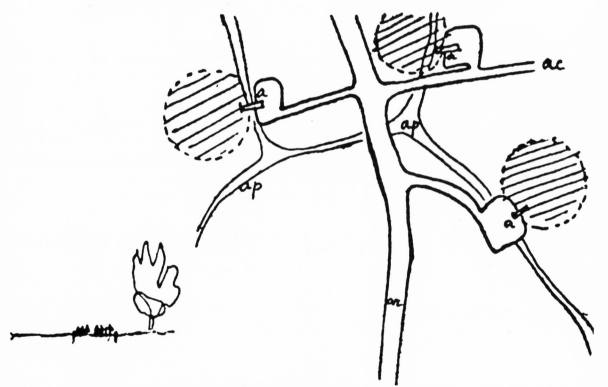

Two independent networks: pedestrian, cars

The fact that the ground is occupied by previously thought-out housing units of suitable size (dwellings with their extensions; places of work; leisure centers) gives us all the elements entering into the traffic problem, which can be broken down into categories:

    1. transit (pedestrians)
    2. patterns of frequentation (pedestrians)
    3. transit (vehicles)
    4. distribution (vehicles)
    5. slow traffic (promenade), pedestrians and vehicles together.

The pedestrian network will be proportioned and laid out in accordance with specific data: width and itineraries.

The traffic of mechanized (high-speed) vehicles follows an imperative rule: the faster the flow of traffic, the straighter the roadway will be and the more sweeping the curves; the edges of the roadway will always be parallel; since flow is to be uninterrupted, no parking will be allowed anywhere along the way; special areas will be set aside for parking, generally at the very foot of each of the buildings to be served.

The highways themselves can have various types of cross section: A, B, C, D, E, etc. (following) correspond to different purposes.

Lastly, where two streams of high-speed traffic come together, they will be channelled along one-way giratory intersections, preferably on more than one level. A whole range of problems, of varying complexity, needs to be solved—single-level on the ground (M) or multi-level (P, R)—in obedience to specific rules, covering all cases from the simplest to the most complicated. Intersections of automobile traffic have given rise to a genuine scientific technique, with nothing arbitrary about it.

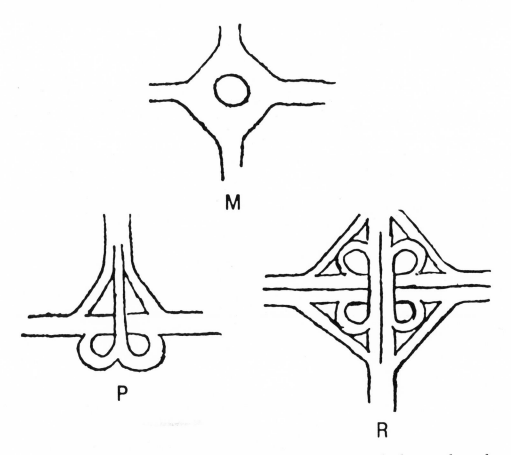

There remains to lay down the rules for running highways through cities and through the countryside.

In those cities which grew up, or were rebuilt, little by little, highways will be a transit phenomenon using the most direct, most simplified network, entirely dependent on the ground-level topography but totally independent of any buildings that might be close by.

These buildings will then be served by a distribution network connected to the transit lanes; each of the ramifications set aside for that
distribution will widen out, at the end, in a parking area atop a garage,
and both of these will be integral parts of the dwelling unit or the work
or leisure-time unit, etc.

Once this is done, the two networks—pedestrian and automobile—
can be used simultaneously.

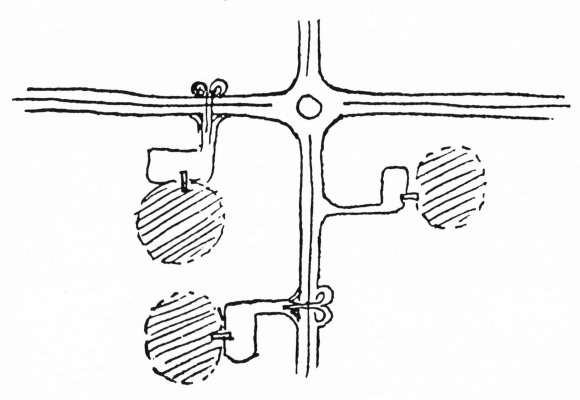

Automobile traffic

Finally, at certain points in the city, there remains to settle the matter
of combined car-and-pedestrian traffic. Slow traffic, pleasure traffic localized around specific points: the city's main public service sectors, department stores, places of entertainment, cafés, theaters, meeting halls of
all kinds, all that inevitably constitutes the goal of the city dweller's daily
outings. It seems only natural to limit the speed of automobile traffic
and keep out heavy trucks. Here the pedestrian will move side by side

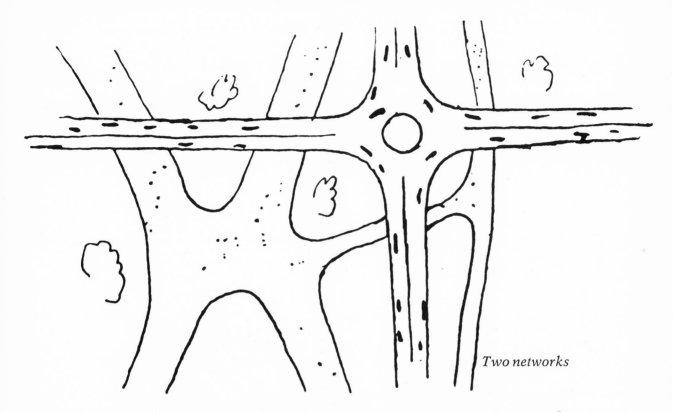

Two networks

with the cars: broad sidewalks, roadways, lawns, flowers and trees, café terraces all on the same level.

Roads outside the city have begun to be organized; thus far, they have taken on two forms.

The first is the big master turnpike connecting two cities by means of a protected roadway free of any interruption. Branch roads are considered subordinate and do not in fact cross it except over bridges or through tunnels. The point at which they do open out onto the highway, which is closed to them by means of a gate, is controlled by a signalman, as is the case with railway grade crossings.

The second form was born in the United States, where it is known as the *parkway*. The idea is to carve a path delicately through the country-side for a set of master lanes which are similarly shielded from any dangerous crossing by means of arrangements on one or more levels. Traffic does not move at the same speed on a parkway as it does on the type of highway described above. The parkway is intended primarily as a channel

for pleasure driving and incorporates a number of landscaping solutions; it has in fact been laid out in terms of plastic beauty. These lanes have a special statute: because they are set aside solely for pleasure driving and sport, no heavy trucks or other types of commercial transportation are allowed to use them. At the end of this chapter we will see how and why they came into being in the area around New York and how they are giving us a glimpse right now into the future of our cities.

Let's sum things up: the sketch we see one paragraph back expresses the harmonious solution found for traffic in a residential zone on a very difficult (very hilly) site.

The overly systematic methods used by today's civil engineers, especially by highway engineers—as expressed by the twin terms, *excavating* and *filling in* (which are exclusive, ruinous, disappointing and nature-destroying)—are going to be able to change. The parkway technique in friendly contact with nature—with the ground and what covers it—becomes a landscaping science. Separating traffic into categories of circulation, making traffic orderly, it spares sites of rustic beauty and thus assures the inhabitants of a residential area that they will find an exceptionally pleasant setting. The site itself is hardly touched whereas, with the methods that are still in use everywhere, our cities are turned into implacable straitjackets of asphalt, concrete and stone.

VERTICAL TYPES OF CIRCULATION

In most of the foreseeable cases, the unit of suitable size, whether conceived as a dwelling or as a place of work or of leisure, will be a direct product of height, the solution being in fact to build upwards instead of sideways, in order to free more land around the building.

This would be merely a fanciful pretension if the slightest flaw remained in the technique of high-rise transportation. But this is not the case. Experiments have been carried out not only in Europe, which is held back by its traditions, but in America too. Anyone who has not seen with his own eyes how elevators are operated in the United States will always fear all the mishaps imaginable.

America solved this problem in twenty years, just as the problem of the engine-heavier-than-air was solved in the same period of time. The figures for 1938 alone are proof in themselves.

In New York, the subway carries six million passengers every day. The buses and trolleys carry three million. The elevators carry fifteen million every day.

Another detail: Rockefeller Center (the latest big New York skyscrapers) has one hundred sixty elevators; each of them travels 750,000 miles—thirty times the circumference of the earth—every year.

The secret to the solution lies in this: American elevators don't know what it is to break down, since they are run solely by professional elevator operators—mechanics.[5]

All it would take to arrive at an overall view of the use of elevators or of their *raison d'être* and the advantages that may be derived from using them would be to word the question this way:

a) Work out the cost of the vertical mile of transportation per person and compare it with the cost of the horizontal mile of transportation per person.

b) Take that difference, which may be in favor of the horizontal mile, and, opposite it, note all the various extra items of expense incurred by virtue of the spreading of the city, the scattering of its population. For instance: cost of laying down roads and keeping them in repair, cost of mechanized means of transport (suburban trains, buses, subways, trolleys, etc.), cost of utility mains (water, gas, electricity, telephone and telegraph lines, etc.); additional expenses affecting dwellings remote from others; lastly, the estimated value of the time spent (lost) in the daily process of getting back and forth.

This is how a verdict will be reached in the trial of the scattered city *vs.* the compact city, and this is how the choice will be made as far as circulation is concerned between two concepts of the way in which progress should be put to use: being able to get about in the city by walking through parks, or having to spend one hour or two or three hours every day in mechanized means of transportation between distant points. The answer that would seem to emerge, of its own accord, is this: men of the machine-age civilization will go about on foot in their re-conceived cities. Alongside the traditional metric scale of measurement used in city-planning projects, machine-age man will introduce another scale: that of *an hour's worth of walking* (3 miles, or 4 kilometers, per hour). Existence of this scale alongside the other will make men stop and think opportunely.

[5] S. Giedion: *Space, Time, Architecture and City Planning*, Harvard University Press, Chap. IX, p. 559.

Landscaping units

The vital role assigned to *natural conditions* has been emphasized throughout this analysis; they are to provide the counterweight needed to offset the artificial factors born of machines.

So it is time to take stock of the *nature-capital* which is available, keep account of the types of nature in stock; nature plays an essential part in the *residence* function (sun, space, greenery). It is present in the *work* function (greenery and sky) as well. It has an outstanding role to play in the *physical and spiritual culture* (sites and landscape) function. It accompanies *circulation* (sites and landscape).

City planning and architecture can bring sites and landscapes into the city or make them into a feature of the city itself, a decisive feature of plastic awareness and sensitivity. A site or a landscape does not exist— except as our eyes see it. The idea, therefore, is to make it visibly present, choosing the best of the whole or the parts of it. This source of inestimable benefit must be grasped. A site or a landscape is made of vegetation seen close up, of stretches of level or uneven terrain, or horizons seen at a distance or right in front of us. Climate places its stamp on the whole, dictating what is fit to survive and develop there. Its presence will always be felt both in what surrounds the constructed thing as a volume and in the reasons which had so much to do with deciding on the very shape of the constructed thing. The sun is in command, again, always, and unity will preside over the laws of nature and the spirit of human undertakings.

The search for units of suitable size has caused the intervention of architectural and city-planning elements, all of them authorized by modern techniques, all created in response to the most legitimate aspirations of human sensitivity, all reliably providing material fulfillment of the most normal needs. Entire, fully described organisms, developing outward from within, genuine biology of cement, stone, iron, glass. Given the pressure being put on us by mechanically-produced speed, a decision is urgently needed: decision to *liberate cities from the stranglehold, the tyranny of streets!* A thing which is possible today.

To get an idea of what a long way we have come, let's take an example. It is drawn from city planning as currently practiced, and, what is more, from the city planning that is fashionable and held up as exemplary to students in schools. It consists of applying the principle not of *dis*memberment but of *re*-memberment (regrouping scattered plots of land) in order to widen streets to a new gauge.

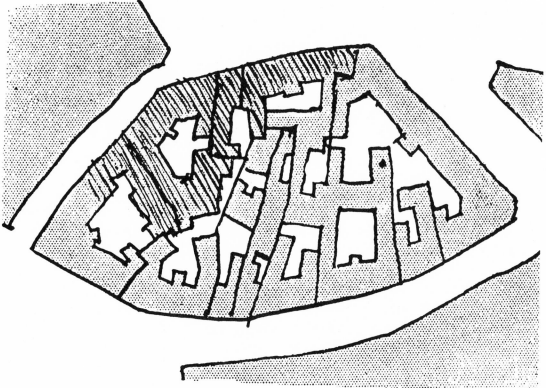

Figure A: a slum block.

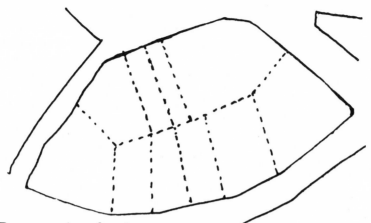

Figure B: regrouping of real estate.

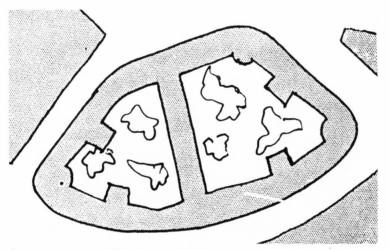

Figure C: new construction arrangement, consisting of
buildings on streets and large courtyards.

Result: 1. The street remains a corridor, the common thoroughfare for pedestrians, cars, buses, trolleys, etc.

2. The façades (their windows) open onto the noise and the dust of the street or the courtyards;

3. dwellings continue to be oriented in an arbitrary way, at the mercy of streets laid out without any obligation to the rule of the sun;

4. greenery is confined to prettying-up courtyards; it has no part in the scenery of the street, and this is a heavy loss to the city;

5. the arrangement chosen overlooks the key matter of "extensions of the dwelling," the key to the housing problem.

Whereas, on the contrary, the situation which results from application of the principles we have been expounding in these pages leads to figure D.

Figure D:

When extended to the other blocks nearby, it spontaneously frees the ground surface and separates traffic into categories, pedestrians and cars. A rational orientation of the dwelling is achieved naturally, and extensions of the dwelling find the necessary space on the ground. The city is gradually transformed, becoming a park.

This example is enough to show the extent of the renewal which architecture and city planning propose here. Once the *tyranny of the street* has been abolished, there is no limit to what we may hope.

In the course of this brief investigation of *units of suitable size*, it has been reassuring to come across certain ideas in the material made available to us that are altogether identical to those which constitute the very armature of our doctrine, ideas held by researchers of all types working at different periods in history.

Hyacinthe Dubreuil tells us how he earnestly studied the *biology of work*. And he points out how closely our doctrine of architecture and city planning is also related to biology, healthy biology, organizing every part of it.

Dr. E. T. Gillard, who compared the wisdom of the West with that of the Orient, appealed to *joy of living* and looked for the superior equations of *harmony* which make the contact between nature and man possible.

Over a hundred years ago, Charles Fourier, first visionary of the machine age, likewise chose *joy of living* as the gauge of his social constructions.

Descartes had opened up a new outlook (modern times) to mankind by expressing the law of universal order. *There is a oneness between the works of nature and the works of the human spirit.*

These biological laws, this constant reference to the life that animates such material things as buildings or city-planning blueprints are also to be found in the life of societies. At the dawn of the machine age, Victor Considérant, who was already concerned with the same problems, said, "Architectonic arrangements vary according to the nature and form of the society whose image they are. In every age they translate the fundamentals that constitute the social state, they are the faithful reflection of them and characterize them beautifully."

Fourier had gone before him: "As it is with societies, so it is with buildings: methods adapted to each social period."

But the time was not ripe in the days of Fourier and Considérant, dreamers, who had written, for instance, that water for household use could be led into each dwelling through metal pipes. Folly!, came the answer: weren't there water carriers (all dying of consumption) who did just that? who, in return for money, would carry water up to the first, the second, even the sixth floor of the house at any hour of the day? And weren't there bath men too, whom tarts and respectable moribund bourgeois could hire to bring a tin tub filled with the necessary hot water right to their homes?

Flights of fancy! . . .

Ordinary mortals are terrified, panic-stricken at the idea of change. They cannot picture themselves shifting from one thing to another. Their fear puts a brake on society.

In America, as the vast territory was little by little taken over, cities were laid out on the grid of roughly 120 meters (400 feet) used by the first colonizers — Spanish, French, Dutch or English. Several centuries later, skyscrapers rearing 600 to 900 feet high line streets which had been intended for the calm movements of men, horses or oxen. New York and Chicago are so bristling, so choked, so tangled that you say to yourself, "There is no cure for such a sickness."

And there is nothing but unspeakable chaos.

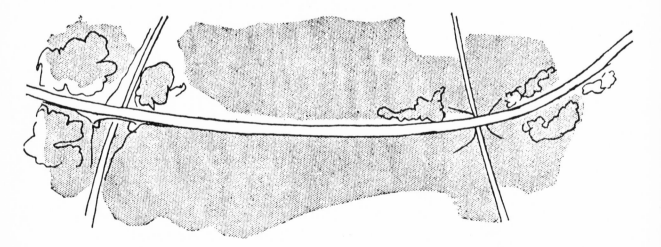

My first impression is that the parkway theory was intended only as a soothing remedy administered to urban populations frantically caught up in the relentless routine of mechanized transportation. It actually affected only the millionaires who lived out in the beautiful Connecticut countryside, north of New York.

This being the case, and Connecticut having been embellished by these superb luxury and pleasure roads, it became possible to observe certain factors concerning the relative hierarchy of the various highway circuits. It was found that the homicidal speed of more than sixty miles an hour necessitated a hierarchical statute of road assignment and inflexible discipline.

One day quite recently, the parkway began to form a belt around the city. The Hudson River edge of New York City was the scene of appalling traffic conflicts — carts coming off the docks, sudden tides of persons and goods coming in and out amidst total confusion at various points along the river bank, as ocean liners berthed or departed . . .

The parkway was put in place, with its different levels for different categories of traffic. Although its layout had been planned from a utilitarian standpoint, it was no less marked by a characteristic concern with gracefulness, with the happy marriage of technique and nature. This Hudson River parkway wrapped a genuine belt of splendor around the flank of the

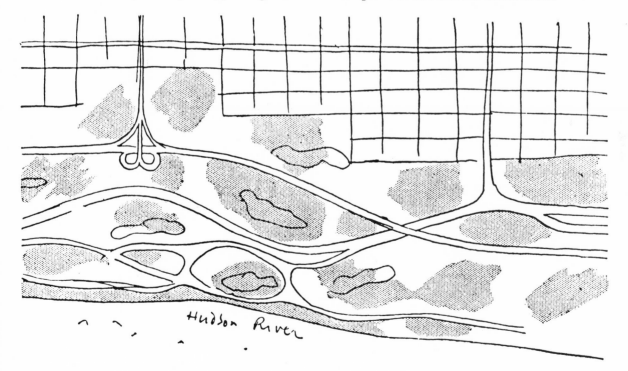

Hudson River

city, expelling disorderly and still precarious harbor installations. And out of the city with its rigid gridiron patterns, its ludicrously throttled circulation systems, forced to follow channels that do not offer any parking facilities, crisscrossed with intersections that are ridiculously close to one another — out of the city, ways of draining off this congestion are already opening onto the parkway. In this urban body, this organism which seemed hopelessly doomed to ossification, paralysis, lo and behold! a new biological element has appeared. It is still only a rim, still no more than a belt around the city, but already feeder roads have established contact with the inner network where, one day, a new sap is bound to rise, and that transformation will equip the city with an authentic system of constructed units beneficial to men.

Paralyzed by its petrified streets, America has discovered the parkway just in time; and Europe, choking and crushed under its heritage of centuries-old cities, has discovered a biological principle which regenerates the constructed volume: the principle of units of suitable size. In his history of architecture, S. Giedion noted, "The parkway is the forerunner of the first necessity in the development of the future town: the abolition of the *rue corridor.*

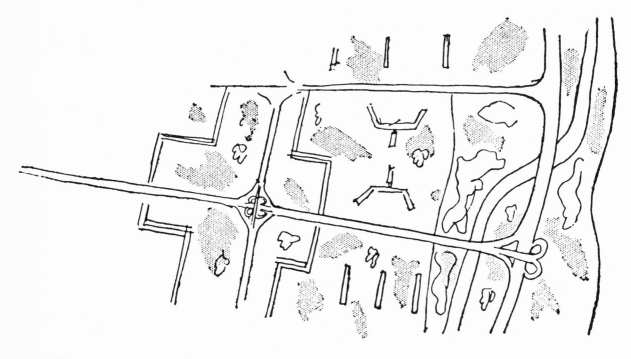

There is no longer any place for the street with its traffic lane running between two rows of houses; it cannot possibly be permitted to persist. And the parkway is the first realized step in this clear separation of traffic and housing. It looks ahead to the time when, after the necessary surgery has been performed, the artificially swollen city will be reduced to its normal size. Then the parkway will go through the city as it does today through the landscape, as flexible and informal as the plan of the American home itself."[6]

[6] See appendix.

CHAPTER 7

Attempt at urbanistic exploration

Building (architecture and city planning) is the faithful reflection of a society. Constructed objects are the most revealing documents about it. But this implies that the times are in full swing. During periods of mutation, much of what has to do with building does not exist except in the precursors' plans. Yet those plans have an absolute value and deserve as much attention as any other examples of buildings already erected, since the many — in fact, the countless — laboratory experiments which have been so many milestones throughout the twelve decades of the first machine age, undeniably form a foundation that will render the super-structure safe.

So it is that at any hour of the day, any point in time, ingenious minds, predisposed to the accomplishment of this task, are in a position to play today's game, in other words, to scout out the pathways of tomor-row which will enable a society to fulfill its mission and earn its daily bread. This is how the flock is being guided. This is how preparations are being made for tomorrow.

The approach being used is a special one. It comes and goes, follow-ing clues along trails that may seem unexpected, paradoxical or even long abandoned, going back through the ages, wandering over geography. With one line, one sketch, it is possible to lay down on a sheet of paper the figurative representation of a thought, a cycle, an era, even one still in the future. The figures form an equation; this graphic algebra has its rules; the velocity of it lets the explorer take giant steps over the under-growth and bare the principle. And so emerge the guidelines of a stage already begun but whose meaning had not been apparent to all. Such and such a development, once considered an accidental happening, appears, on the contrary, as a distinct phenomenon, revealing the conditions in which it emerged, assuming its contiguities with existing things some of which have every reason to remain and others to fade away — leaving room for nothings which will become great things, vital elements of the imminent life.

If a serious attempt to ponder the problems of aviation had been made fifty, or even just twenty or thirty years ago, couldn't it have guided a whole swarm of decisions which had, instead, to be taken amidst the perilous improvisation of sentiment or interest or panic?

In all of its conceivable circumstances, the world of building is infinitely more definable, graspable. Attempts at reasoning can be based on its various realities — constructional, geographic, social, economic. Besides, with any mutation, there is one outstanding, eminently favorable hour. There is nothing fanciful about believing that that hour is striking today, the hour when we absolutely must look ahead.

Let's take, as our vantage point, the most impartial sort of generality: a wedge of territory large enough to contain the diversified features of a continent. Here we have a barely suggested Europe, nothing more, with a seashore up there at the top, a seashore at the bottom, an ocean to the west, a Black Sea on the other side . . . The watershed has created natural pathways. Men and things naturally go down to the sea.

But an increasing population has filled the empty spaces of the territory. The Americas were discovered and also, more recently, steam engines. The silence of the West came to be filled with great clamors and life came throbbing against the threshold of the ocean; steamships created this new state of affairs. Eastward, railway tracks formed a trail for locomotives, but the gait of camels pulling caravans in the sands or the steppes, up to the Bosporus, ceased.

One day, the Atlantic Ocean-Black Sea canal can be dug, feasible example of a passageway for raw materials, possible site of their processing all along its banks.

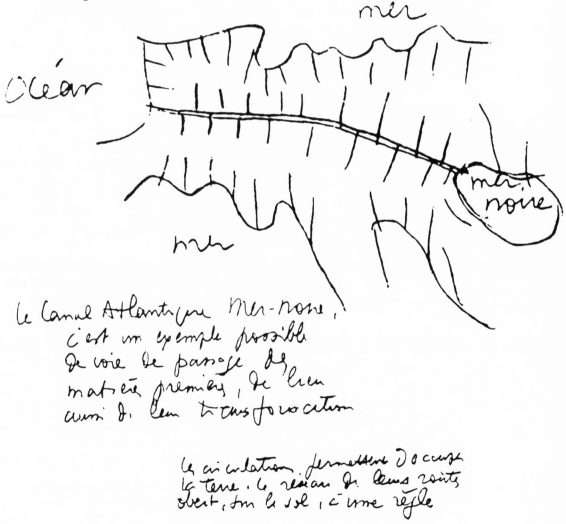

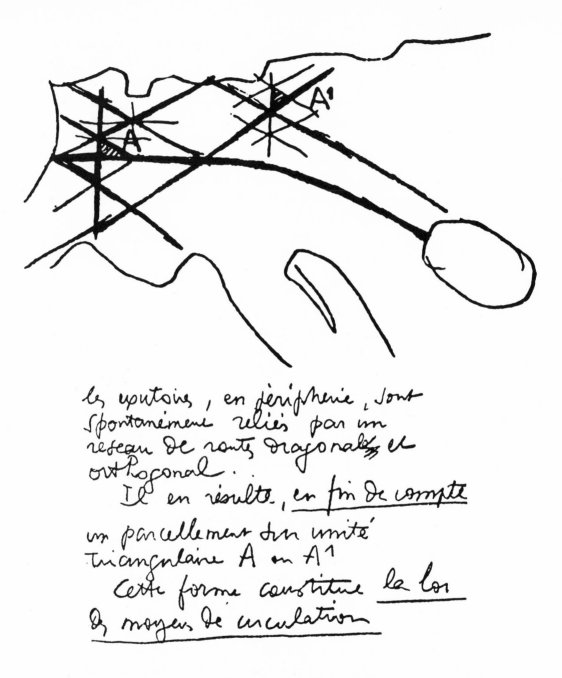

les exutoires, en périphérie, sont
spontanément reliés par un
réseau de routes diagonales et
orthogonal.
Il en résulte, en fin de compte
un parcellement d'un unité
Triangulaire A en A¹
Cette forme constitue la loi
des moyens de circulation

A new, complementary irrigation channel for the continent, pregnant with consequences, with promise and with hazards. Pathways of circulation make it possible to occupy the land. A formidable canal, filled with the lifeblood of today and tomorrow — one cannot hope to bring such a canal into the picture and do it with impunity.

Around the periphery, starting from the outlets, great pathways of penetration have been or will be created, pathways of potential action and business, tracing crisscrossing diagonals and diamond shapes.

Let's look closely at the texture of this network. The diagonals and the orthogonals (which is what any network boils down to) form intersections, the last of which enclose a right-angled triangle (A) or any other kind of triangle (A'), depending ultimately on whether the pathways of communication meet to form an eight-pointed or a six-pointed star.

As a result, the territory is parcelled into basic triangular units, A or A'. This consequence would seem to exemplify the law of *patterns of movement.*

Any territory that is sufficiently vast can be expressed by a lap-like valley held in between slopes and opening onto a more or less extensive plain, aligned on a seaboard. The slopes, in turn, are divided by the same phenomenon, this time forming valleys of varying sizes, to the bottoms of which streams or brooks descend; and, all gathered into a single river, they are led into the sea.

The hilly zone forms the region of flowing water.

Far, far back in the past, men installed the waterwheel to drive the mill and the fuller and the forge; the nailworks, the foundry and the locksmithery were grouped around this distribution point of energy drawn from nature. Industry naturally took up its abode there.

Iron is to be found everywhere in the mountains, in ore deposits that are more or less rich; the forests provide the fuel.

Industry settles where the energy of flowing water can be used.

Eventually the forests are exhausted or threatened with exhaustion. The law makes it forbidden to touch them from now on. Industries located in valleys are dying.

The unforeseen event occurs: the discovery of the steam engine. The steam engine comes into the valley, alongside the mill, and creates modern industry. Then the electric motor, in turn, supplants steam. And suddenly, arbitrarily, paradoxically, dangerously, modern industries will find that they are badly located — located contrary to the dictates of common sense — and so give rise, all around them, to a series of contradictions, paradoxes, disastrous or merely disturbing anomalies.

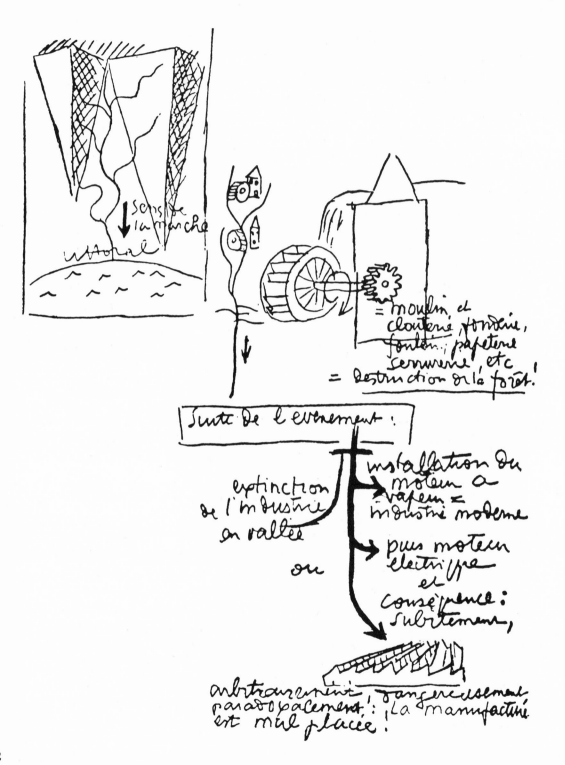

Certain industries set up in valleys are badly located.

For other, equally accidental reasons, other industries have invaded the cities or placed a belt around them, bringing about the great discomfort we feel today.

Let's continue our exploring.

The dusk of one civilization and the dawn of another were marked by mechanical inventions. The age-old habit of one speed, 3 miles per hour (the gait of man, horse, ox), abruptly shifted to 30 or 60 or even 300 miles per hour for the transportation of persons and products, and to the unlimited speed of telegraph, telephone, radio for the conveyance of ideas (information, orders, supervision).

The purpose of our exploration is to discern, from amidst the present confusion, the efficient, economic and elegant process governing the regular acts of a society extending over a territory. A measuring instrument should be designated by which to appraise[7] the value of the solutions that are found. The ASCORAL viewpoint will be the following:

Efficiency considered, not in relation to *money* but in relation to *man*, man being installed in his environment, the environment specific to his action, his existence.

What is actually involved is the occupation of the ground for various purposes: to produce and to trade in order to consume (feed, clothe and amuse).

PRODUCTION

---

a) Products of the earth — agriculture;
b) Products of machines — industry. Processing;
c) Trade and distribution — commerce.

OCCUPATION OF THE GROUND

A) Farms, villages and rural centers
B) Industrial cities
C) Cities of public and private administration
　　　　of trade,
　　　　of the intellect and of art,
　　　　of government.

---

[7] Thesis of Dr. E. T. Gillard.

Thus, according to our yardstick (man, the welfare of man), the mutation of the present day has to do with a revision and a harmonization of *living conditions.*

	Food supply	the economic
Living conditions	Housing (and its extensions)	the patriarchal
	Sociability	the spiritual

This three-column summary contains the very elements that make up a spiritual and technical doctrine of city planning. The choice of favorable living conditions is the end purpose assigned to the humblest of our undertakings, the product of the action balance sheet, and ultimately: joy of living, or not. The following three factors cover (as far as we city planners are concerned) a part of the agrarian and industrial problems, so that the economic element is at stake. First of all, food supply, which is connected with the stomach — that is, with the human being as creature, with his most imperative day-to-day impulse. The dwelling and its extensions entail perpetuation of the species — pre-birth, birth, eugenics, child-rearing. An essential share of sensitivity and instinctive forces, the patriarchal feeling, is involved. Sociability concerns groups, whether small or enormous, independent or united, which can be led to harbor feelings of mutual respect, esteem and even love just as easily as feelings of hate, mistrust and rivalry. Here is the occasion for arousing altruism, which is the motivating force behind great and magnificent efforts, which in turn generate enthusiasm and pride.

Wrought to their highest degree, these *living conditions* will unceasingly fill our minds and ensure that the three great animating elements — the economic, the patriarchal and the spiritual — are kept present in our work.[8]

Now let's go back to the three purposes for which the ground is occupied: *a*) land; *b*) industry; *c*) trade.

THE RURAL UNIT

Let's explore the agrarian phenomenon in terms of the *law of speeds.*

Why should we submit to the law of speeds? Because the various and contradictory proposals put forward for the reawakening of agriculture

[8] Dr. E. T. Gillard, *"Synthèse Universelle."*

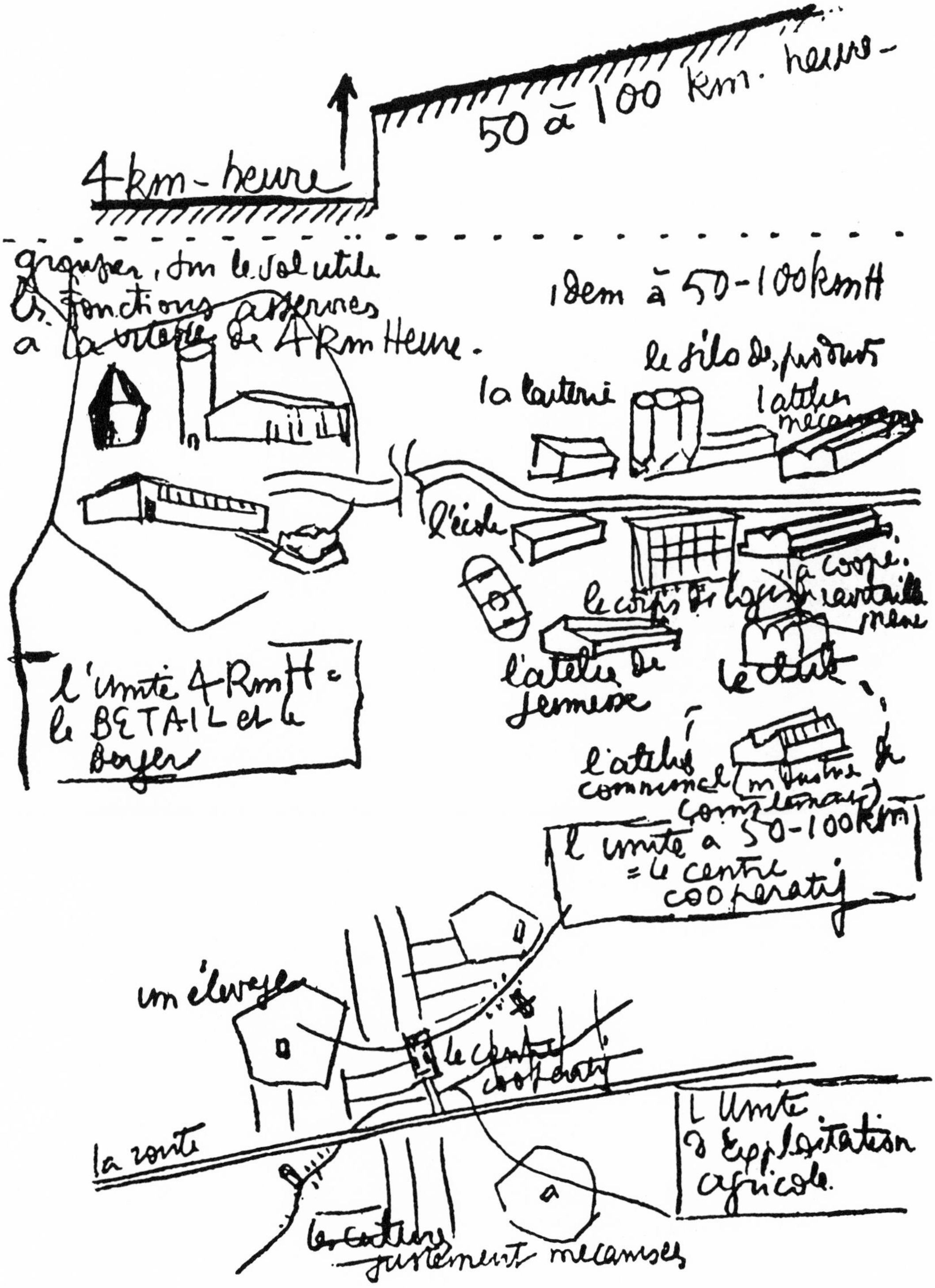
50 à 100 km. heure-
4 km-heure
idem à 50-100 kmH
l'unité 4 kmH = le BETAIL et le berger
l'unité à 50-100 km = le centre coopératif
un élevage
la route
L Unité d'Exploitation agricole

are so knotted up in the hopeless network of individual cases that they seem to be lacking one undeniable factor. Here let us institute the revolutionary event itself.

Let's recognize which aspects of agrarian life are strictly (and without any possibility of change) subject to the speed of 3 miles per hour. Furthermore, let's acknowledge that once the hard-surfaced road, which can be used by mechanized vehicles (the motor and all the consequences of it) is laid down in the countryside, it is (or shortly will be) the magic wand which, alone, can solve the problem created by the factors shown in the picture above.

Once we have got this far, then we distinguish those elements in the agrarian unit (the farm) which are subject to the law of 3 miles per hour: the cattle and the herdsmen. The facilities they use: the stables, the haystack (or the hayloft), the forage silo and the kitchen-storehouse for cattle feed, and housing for the herdsmen. Their territory: the pasturelands.

Then let's distinguish what already benefits, or is about to benefit, from the law of speeds of 30 to 60 miles an hour. This means the rural (or cooperative) center that has been talked about for such a long time and groups the dairy, the farm produce silo, the machine shop and the hangar for farm machinery and tools, and finally, the workshop (or small mill) for related industry.

This also means the main dwelling, the food cooperative, the school, the crafts shop for young people and the club, with its common playing fields.

These rural events are not imminent but, milestones to the future as they inevitably are, they give us more than a glimpse of the type of land redistribution capable of making peasant life flourish once again. First of all, in a place determined by natural geography, the pastureland(s). Then, close to the most important route (but not directly alongside it), the rural center. Finally, the fields with their judicious use of machines (single- or multi-crop farming). But the drawing on the preceding page gives us a more exact prefiguration of the possible development of agriculture.

One village, or two or three, or more. The church, the cemetery, the farms that are still in good shape remain; the farms that are collapsing from old age will not be rebuilt. The villages will be the way stations along the path of mutation.

The rural center.

Pastureland(s), with the stables and related structures.

Vegetable gardens (produce for local consumption or for sale).

Orchards.

Grains, roots and tubers, the vines, etc., depending on the region.

Various smooth-surfaced roads.

The water tower, the center of civilian and civic forces in the heart of the cooperative center.

The industrial city

Let's take a look at the industrial city, where raw materials are transformed.

In this study we have taken inventory of the units of work, and we have recognized the specific forms they take: workshops, mills, factories. They are situated as close as possible, of course, to the passageways used by raw materials and goods.

The means of transportation to be borne in mind are: waterways, roads and railways, either independent of one another, or paired, or, better still, all three grouped in places determined by the geography of the region or the country or even a whole group of countries — a decision on which light will be shed by the human geography covered in the next chapter.

The waterway, which is the means best suited to modern heavy transportation, harmoniously brings together two phenomena that had been antagonistic until now, and one of which — industry — had lived voraciously at the expense of the other — agriculture.

The problem, we repeat, is one of living conditions, the object being to introduce better living conditions.

BAD conditions now obtaining in industrial life:

a) tumult and disorder;

b) complete absence of *natural conditions;*

c) discouraging remoteness of residential zones (recourse daily to mechanized transportation, costly for the user and ultimately ruinous for society);

d) because of today's radio-concentric industrial cities, an abundant labor market — and the consequence of that: instability and nomadic life for working people;

e) desertion of the countryside.

GOOD conditions to be made paramount in industrial life:

a) orderliness and cleanliness;

b) reinstatement of *natural conditions;*

c) proximity of places of residence and elimination, as a result, of commuters' long, daily to-and-fro;

d) elimination of nomadic life by timely installation of the meticulously adapted facilities composing the linear industrial city;

e) real and harmonious contact with peasant life.

An exceptionally fortunate example of living conditions, fulfilling its economic, patriarchal and spiritual trilogy, the machine-age society dominates its machines and is master of its industry. And the industrial cities which, until now, have been scenes of ugliness and tumult, become places propitious for optimistic work ("green factories").

The figure at the top of the next page shows:

1. the canal or river;

2. the railway;

3. the highway;

4. the workshops, mills and factories;

5. the green protecting zone;

A) the horizontal garden-city residential area;

B) the vertical garden city (apartment building equipped with communal services);

C) the semi-rural homes;

D) various extensions of the dwelling: schools, young people's crafts shops, clubs, sports, etc.

Here we go to the heart of the problem. While industry develops to the best of its potential, the dwelling, in turn, finds its optimum solution. Variety in the choice of a dwelling (whether definitive or temporary place of residence), depending on age, marital status, specific taste or temperament and a thousand other influential factors, corresponds to every manifestation of individual personality.

But other possibilities will become apparent soon, as we go ahead with our exploration.

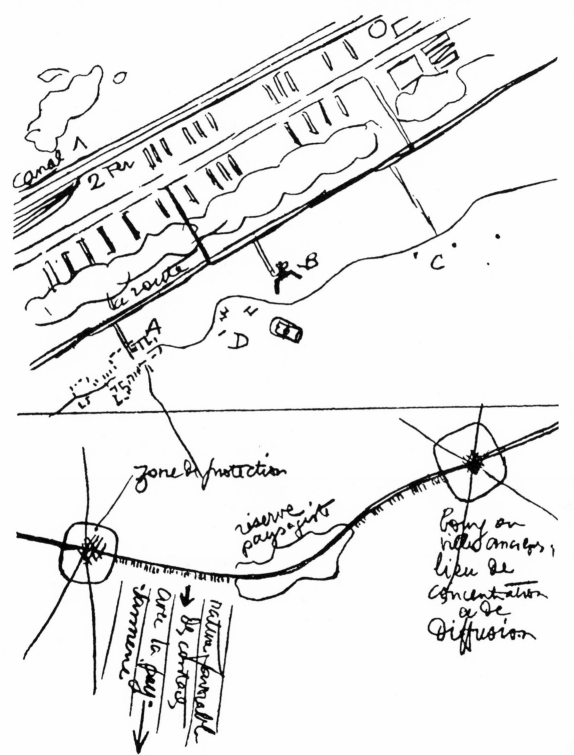

The linear industrial city has its specific biology. It is not a ribbon of unlimited length. It is naturally brought into contact with distance (the region and the country) and with time (the past, the present and the future); and in fact when we begin to look for its points of thoroughfare, we are led back to the waterway and the overland road, and even to the railway. The rational itinerary, which we are looking for here, will coincide with or follow the old routes, for the pathways of history are the products of geography.

Thus, the linear city will be sectioned wherever it runs into old centers built up at the points where roadways intersect (market town or old city, point of focus and of radiating influence); these are the turntables, seats of trade. They will become outlets for the linear city, letting it reach far and deep into the country; contact established with society.

The picture shows another wholesome contact: regular, side-by-side contact with the land; the peasantry within walking distance; direct interchange between an industrial society carrying on its activity all along a certain line, and an immediately contiguous peasant society. What kind of contact? Not a confusion, a fallacious attempt to mix two orders of things that may be governed by rules that do not allow the one to pass into the other within the daily allotment of twenty-four solar hours: the factory worker governed by the daily solar laws of *twenty-four hours,* the peasant by the *yearly* solar law (365 days and 4 seasons). Rules which clearly imply two profoundly different types of conduct, difficult to blend into one.

Contacts will be of a social and not a professional nature. It is not the hands which will meet in a gesture that would be nothing more than competition, but the heads, in a movement which will be an act of neighborliness. In this way a oneness of thinking will grow up that will cease to make eternal adversaries of the peasant and the factory worker.

The image also reveals another decision of capital importance: the linear industrial city will extend along *only one side* of the passageways (canal, road or railway) and not along both. Otherwise those passageways would be incessantly interrupted and each interruption would be a latent hindrance. The other side belongs, on the contrary, to the land, to the rural life.

The linear city will have the most perfected, longitudinal mechanized means of transport for people, materials and products. Means of movement belonging to all, a common and possibly free service, distinct from all of the networks crisscrossing the country.

At either end of each section of the linear city a protecting zone is planned, a stretch of territory held in reserve.

In the middle of the linear shape of the industrial city, another reserve; this one, landscaped, will serve various purposes, immediate or future.

Here we are at one end of an element of the linear city, where it would run into a radio-concentric population center if it weren't for the precautionary isolating zone that is set aside. The linear city may react on the population center — and vice versa — in very different ways depending on their relative size. They cannot fail to react in positive ways if the contacts between the two centers have been carefully prepared for.

The existing nucleus, the radio-concentric population center, may number 10,000 inhabitants — or a million. Customs, intensity, "social voltage" peculiar to each case.

At the top of the next figure, "IP" designates the precautionary isolating zone where a great many important events — or none at all — can take place. By this I mean that this large area of available space, covered with fields, meadows, orchards or woods offers exceptionally favorable conditions for the installation of such annexes of the linear industrial city as special technical schools and laboratories, headquarters of trade or professional unions, as well as facilities that encourage the cultivation of mind and body: stadiums for the big, spectacular contests, libraries, theaters — in short, all the elements of an intellectual center to be used as suits each individual case. The old population center (large town or city) can benefit from part of these new institutions and thus experience the happy effects of reinvigoration. The reverse is also true: with its mighty spiritual potential, the population center allows the linear city to take advantage of its facilities and of its most vivid traditions.

To sum up, we can say that points CV', CL and FL will cohabit without friction or antagonism; each of them will contribute its particular energy and react gently on the other two.

It should be noted that, under the effects of their reciprocal relationship, the industrial city has become a "linear satellite" of the radio-concentric population center; this system replaces that of the radio-concentric satellites proposed by certain present-day theoreticians and which, upon closer examination, appears to be only a decoy, a dangerous measure.

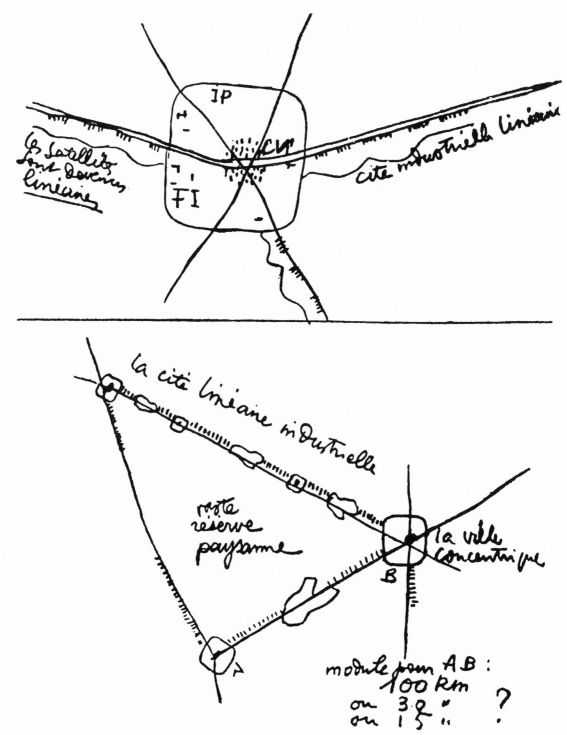

les satellites
sont devenus
linéaires

IP

CV

FI

cité industrielle linéaire

la cité linéaire industrielle

reste
réserve
paysanne

la ville
concentrique

B

A

module pour AB :
100 km
ou 30 "
ou 15 " ?

The conclusion emerges: all along its most authentic pathway of com-munications, the linear industrial city stretches, possibly punctuated now and again by the intermediary towns. It ends at the point where the road-ways cross, in the radio-concentric city.

Suppose we observe the rule governing the meeting points of routes. The resulting figure is a triangle, and in that triangle peasant life is contained.

Harmonious occupation of the ground is achieved in a spirit of mutual respect, on the part of both peasantry and industry. Yet a big decision re-mains to be taken, a decision portentous with consequences for the vitality of the country and affecting the quality of its social make-up: how large should the network that is proposed here — the triangle containing peasant life — be? Will the legs of the triangle be 10 miles long, or 20, or 60? This is what the question boils down to: alongside a perfected, har-monious, happy industrial society, is it necessary to maintain a consid-erable reserve of land?

The figure back on page 85 showed that the peasantry could be wrested from the loneliness of its farms or the mediocrity of its hamlets, and that a spirit of quality would be created by new arrangements — a spirit of the same value and the same voltage as, although fundamentally differentiated from, the spirit stemming from the organization of proc-essing industries so as to form linear cities. The land reserves can be extensive, that is, the container-triangle can be very large. The intense and living breath of life will enter it and remain in it.

This brings us to the end of our first urbanistic exploration. It has made us discover valid rules governing the occupation of the ground, rules fully capable of guiding minds and providing judicious advice to those who, every day, take or will have to take the countless big or little decisions — until at last, someone has made living realities out of the technical realities incorporated in the plans.

CHAPTER 8
Occupying the ground

The hour of mutation seems to have struck — mutation by which the machine-age society is going to equip itself with the facilities needed for its equilibrium.

The human anthill has been knocked apart on a number of occasions, each of which has engendered the one following, so that now its tenants go tearing about on badly occupied ground. Everything is called into question — the site itself as well as the size of groupings and the order in which they occur. The disarray is great enough, the confusion obvious enough, the menace and the uneasiness undeniable enough so that a spirit of overall effort can now intervene, reading the situation, gripping the factors involved and shaping, for our edification and for the guidance of our gestures shortly to come, constructed beings, concrete biological systems that may be theoretical but are so steeped in the virtualities of the present that they constitute the very goals toward which our society will strive, in time and space — taking the time it takes, achieving more or less ideal purity, depending on whether the winds are blowing from the right direction or not.

Starting with the needs and the dealings of a mechanized society, we will take a new look at the occupation of the ground. Given the nature of modern tasks (means and duties), three realities of human groupings will stand out, depending on the type of daily work and undertakings, depending on the rules of rational life, depending on the rules of the human spirit and natural harmony, depending on the equilibrium to be achieved between the effort and its reward — all of these things which are nothing other than the successive hours, days and years of a life intelligently adapted to the conditions that surround us and genuinely manage our lives.

These three groupings depend on the sort of work men do.

1) Work on the land will necessitate the *unit of agricultural activity (the farm)*.

2) That which transforms raw materials will give rise to industrial cities—the *linear cities*.

3) The work of distribution in connection with trade and exchanges, administrative work, mental work, the work of government, reclassifying the *radio-concentric cities* in merged or diversified forms.

Three fundamental units distributed over the ground in obedience to rules stemming from nature itself and which can be clearly discerned. Once this is done, the traditional truths, which are lost today, will be retrieved; the defects, deformations and flaws whose weight strangles or overcomes us will be tossed aside. Finally, a step forward will be taken, bringing man back into agreement with the way his own mind works, placing him at ease and at rest within the grand and masterly architecture of the natural laws, *natural conditions*. Their presence here will no longer mean the crushing archaeological torpor of crumbling arches but rather, the enveloping warmth, the huge, sonorous and harmonious hull of a full ship well-built from contemporary facts. Nature, cosmos and man brought into agreement — ease of gestures and thoughts, acts and conduct. Harmony which must be achieved by the machine-age civilization that is squashed and bruised and torn today by stupor and stupidity.

These three types of grouping — the farm-unit activity, the linear city, the radio-concentric city — constitute the by-laws of present-day society.

a) The country is patterned all over with the points of intersection between the routes and pathways born of geography and history. Predestined points that men naturally took over in order to meet their fate by building their cities there. But disproportion began to appear. These four-pointed or six-pointed stars distribute the human substance (men and thoughts) all over the territory, carrying out *distribution, trade* in the most economical and the most efficient way. What can be distributed, traded? Authority, the influence and the concentration of it; *city of government* (public administration, offices). Thought, the fruit of solitary meditation, confrontation and discussion: *city of thought, city of light*. Goods and money; *trading cities*.

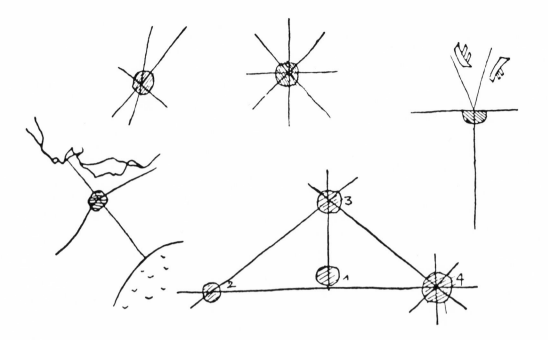

b) The transformation of raw materials wherever energy is available (sturdy arms, the wind, flowing water) and wherever there is a passageway for or accumulation of raw materials.

A certain unchanging context conditioned the acts of earlier millennia of countless generations, imposing an impassive rate of speed upon the universe: the speed at which a man, a horse or an ox walks: 3 miles per hour.

Goods were carried:

      along an overland road,

      along relatively precarious inland waterways (rivers, then canals),

      over the seas, by sailing vessels.

Therefore it was difficult to accumulate raw materials in one place; at the same time they were distributed badly, or scantily, at rates of speed altogether unsuited to land and sea distances. Little movement of raw materials; consequently, few goods in circulation. The industrial city did not in fact exist, but only workshops, mills, set up where labor was to be found, as well as a food supply and a portion of the consumers — in the concentric cities.

First steam, then electricity brought industry into the nineteenth cen-

La cité-linéaire industrielle

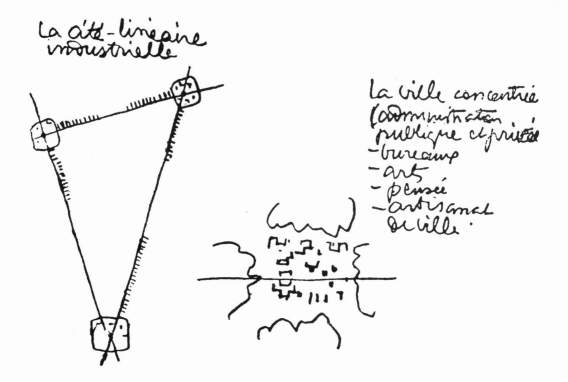

*La ville concentrée
(administration
publique et privée)
- bureaux
- arts
- pensée
- artisanat
de ville.*

*les unités,
D'exploitation agricole
avec "industrie De
complément"*

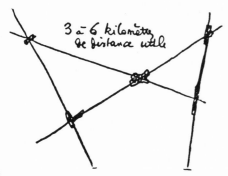

*3 à 6 kilomètres
de distance utile*

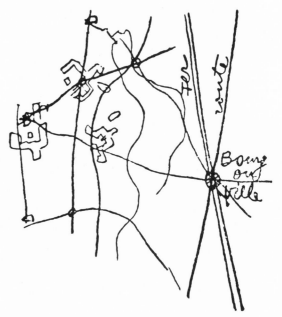

tury once and for all and multiplied by twenty the rate of speed at which products were carried (railways, steamships, mechanized traction on smooth-surfaced roads, then — twentieth century — aviation). Electricity meant the limitless speed of information, order-giving and supervision — telegraph, telephone, radio. The volume of raw materials, the volume of goods, the volume of orders given swelled prodigiously, dramatically, amidst anarchy, negligence, arbitrary will, without guidance. Without any reason the earth is flooded with goods, offers and orders — or suffers a drought of them. In the reigning confusion, greed flourishes at ease, the exploiters and the exploited become enemy classes, and unhappiness settles in deep: chaotic and dangerous concentration in the cities, and the rural regions abandoned.

Thus, for the negative and harmful reasons which have been explained above and for positive reasons which suffice, at this point in our examination, to situate a point of view, the industrial cities, scenes of transformation of raw materials, will be erected where the goods go by, all along the channels of communication. They will be the only tolerable satellite cities, satellites withdrawn from the concentric phenomenon and made subject, instead, to the law of the continuous line; thus making it possible for fertile contact to be established between the places of accumulation and distribution, on the one hand, and the innumerably scattered plots of land all over the territory, the natural points of overflow of rural life. Linear phenomenon which is confirmed by an experiment in human geography.

c) Until this twentieth century, rural life was spared the consequences of speeds twenty times faster than before. Part of it, though, did feel the influence of the railways. But it was the smooth-surfaced road, the combustion engine and the automobile (newspapers, magazines, radio and films, gramophone records and dance halls) which irrigated the land, sowing an unexpected ferment: the attraction of the cities.

Only that same phenomenon of opposing speeds: 3 miles per hour and 60 miles per hour, will be capable of solving the crisis of hegemony which has developed between city and countryside.

For the moment, we will be content here to stick close to this question of different speeds, which is both the cause of the disorder and the appropriate tool for reestablishing order.

The village is the natural human grouping, and it fits in with a nation-wide administration. Here we have the rural village. As long as the prevailing speed was 3 miles per hour, over rugged roads (the horse or the ox as the pulling power) and depending on the nature of the ground (topography or climate), the influence of each village and therefore its contents were clearly conditioned by the limited possibilities for transportation within the solar day of twenty-four hours. Then come the smooth-surfaced road and the automobile engine — i.e., speeds of 30 to 60 miles per hour; from now on, the radius of influence of the village can increase greatly and so, as a result, can its contents. This can imply the merger of several communities around a new nucleus, regenerator of the rural life: the cooperative center. The cultivation of crops, benefiting from the smooth road and the engine, will use completely new methods and be in harmony with the rhythm and with the universal spirit. But although the new speed of 30 to 60 miles per hour tends toward a new harmony in the distribution of labor and the gathering together of products, the age-old speed of 3 miles per hour will still continue to reign over one specific area of the farm unit: the shepherd and his flock. So that the land will be regrouped in such a way as to include, on the one hand, the pasturelands with their flocks, their herdsmen and their stables and, on the other, the rural center with the produce silo, the dairy, the workshop and the machine and toolshed, the food cooperative, housing for the peasant families, the club and its intellectual and sports facilities.

Decision which sheds light to a singular extent on the peasant problem, clearing the way of the parasites placed there and supported by the mass of people secretly introduced into this very complex and particular whole — defenders of private interests — or worse, writers on holiday who sharpen their pens on mossy rooftops and worm-eaten beams and wail disconsolately over the disappearance of thatched roofs on the sheepfolds.

CHAPTER 9
WE ARE NOT TALKING ABOUT PRECONCEIVED IDEAS

Not once anywhere in this study have we been talking about preconceived ideas, about things of which one says: this is how it is because this is how it has always been — an academic notion of values which plunges us constantly into the confusion that stems from lack of foresight (or refusal to see). Nothing has the right to be rejected in the name of custom; new organisms, corresponding to new functional requirements (which may well be essentially permanent) must be allowed to come to life and develop. What we are entitled to demand is health — healthy, sound solutions. But alas(!), the passions (to tack a noble label onto what in fact are senility and sterility) do not hesitate to plot crimes against society (crimes against thought, against technology, against dreams, against poetry), and the victims are not those satisfied, fulfilled persons whom the thrust of modern times has awakened out of their habits. No, the victims are the humble. Horrid selfishness, voracious interests raise a hue and cry, create a certain atmosphere, supply a certain special type of literature penned by "troubadours" humbly devoted to their daily newspaper stint, writers ignorant of what they write about, not the least bit anxious to investigate or obtain accurate information, determined not to alter a single facet of a viewpoint which is bread and butter to them.

These problems are severe, and not everyone is capable of judging them. But heavens, how well he talks, this Mr. Everyman who's to be found in newspapers throughout the country! To back him up, he calls on Montesquieu, La Palisse, Ronsard, Watteau, and Mr. (average or what-have-you) Frenchman. Rhetoric going back to the *grand siècle*, complete with periods and cadence: rules of comfort, law of proportions, mystery of "the number" with infinite modulations.

"No matter what one does, a man's dwelling has something of a temple about it, something sacred. Here is where he venerates his ancestors, pursues his dreams, and where always, obscurely, he tries to find his gods. Societies in ancient times and in the Middle Ages had understood that very well. For them, architecture was a language expressing relationships between the equilibrium of stone and that of the soul. Accordingly, they demanded of this great art that it be not only a matter of knowledge but more: a matter of wisdom." (Mr. Raymond Cristoflour)

Sitting back in the comfort of their newspaper column, they spread panic and doubt in terms like those and create that negative mentality that has so successfully pushed the peasant below his real level and beyond the pale of his tradition.

At the other extreme, there are some people who are so impatient to see things get under way that they think they can make events happen sooner by conducting surveys or public opinion polls, framed like this: "Shall France accomplish its architectural revolution?" The question is put to "anonymous" — but it is also asked of several leading, and perspicacious, figures who are interviewed on their own home ground. Disappointing experiment as far as modern painting or modern poetry or music is concerned. The theme that concerns us — i.e., building — is a technical one, but we have acknowledged that it is linked at the same time to the very depths of consciousness. In which case replies express a sentimental reaction shored up by technological information which is inadequate, faulty or even downright wrong. The reason is that the question is put concerning objects planned for the future, and the only thing about them that already exists is proof, in the form of the laboratory work already mentioned — hundreds of fragmentary, isolated attempts scattered over the last hundred years. The people who are questioned are unaware, or are not fully aware, of them; their reasoning is full of mistakes, their conclusion erroneous. An opinion poll is equally dangerous because the objects it covers are the two terms of a comparison, one of which is *known* (the object which is customarily used) while the other is *unknown* (the object which is proposed). The result can be distorted as much in one direction as in the other, depending on whether the spirit behind it is conservative or innovative. One typical proof of this was the very recent reply made by Auguste Lumière—a touching reply because of the care that went into it, a generous reply on the part of a great and wise man of eighty having felt that it was his duty to give young people —in this instance, a student journal called *L'Echo des Etudiants*—the benefit of his experience. But a thoroughly harmful reply because it is based on the most inaccurate information, and all the more disappointing because signed by the author of *Les Fossoyeurs du Progrès* (*The Grave-diggers of Progress*). It boils down to this: Auguste Lumière rejects high-rise buildings for residential purposes because of the example offered by New York. And yet the question put to him specifically concerned the adoption of apartment buildings 165 feet tall overall in order to replace the buildings now in use which stand 100 or 115 feet tall (at the highest point of the roof). Auguste Lumière argued against this on the basis of the American skyscraper which stands a thousand feet tall, has never been designed for residential purposes but only for offices, and is placed right at the edge of old streets or avenues, blocking traffic on them completely. Wary of the city-planning catastrophe that New York represents, Auguste Lumière recommends that France adopt the individual family bungalow scattered over the countryside and so implying the systems of communication that that would require. In other words, this wise man is proposing to reinstate the experience of the past half century that has led cities down a blind alley and led the societies that live in them into the most alarming kind of confusion.

This *lack* of information is to be found among the important figures who would seem to be the logical choice for taking decisions in this sphere —ministers, high officials, directors of leading national institutes, etc. . . .

The problem goes beyond the scope of a mere living room chat. Here is where ASCORAL outlines the whole set of themes that are open to debate. The first hundred years of the machine age brought the engineer to the fore, conferring more and more power upon him. While this particular branch of mental discipline was flourishing, another branch, the architects, began to wither away—abandoned, rejected by life. Yet the time for general construction will come soon; and whereas once upon a time the architect was supreme, now, faced with the new tasks introduced by the machine-age civilization, he will have to accept the presence on either side of him of two sources of knowledge: the city planner and the engineer. Architect, city planner, engineer—a trilogy calling for a unitary statute. Here is a preamble to such a statute (it dates back to February 1941):

Preamble to a builder's statute
THE PLANNERS ARE TECHNICIANS

Administrators — Architects — City planners — Engineers

1.   The construction of any object calls upon the science of man and the science of materials—the architect and the engineer —to a degree or degrees which can vary infinitely.

a) Any object that is constructed is a reflection of the human consciousness.

b) It is an expression of the laws of gravity and of the strength of materials.

2.   Both types of action together affect a set of objects that involve a large portion of human activity: havens, places of shelter for thought, for institutions, for human beings and for things. And which also involve what links these havens to one another: circulation.

The places of shelter for thought are:

....
....
....

The places of shelter for institutions are:

....
....
....

The places of shelter for human beings are:

....
....
....

The places of shelter for things are:

....
....
....

Circulation means travel on overland roads
              on waterways.
              by rail.
              by air.

3. This vast program requires strict and ever more accurate specialization. It can no longer be conceived and put into action by a single brain working alone.

In each of the many sectors that go to make up this program, technique and art are indissolubly linked to form a unified whole but in quantities which differ depending on whether demands are made almost completely on art and imagination or on the ability to compute and plan.

4. The different forms of intelligence and sensitivity compose an endlessly diversified pattern—on the one hand, appreciation of the most noble plastic forces; on the other, appreciation of the subtleties of the inner structure of matter.

So let us take the intellectual capacities as they are available and line them up alongside the tasks to be accomplished, and in the name of effectiveness, let us call upon forms of intelligence and forms of sensitivity which are in harmony each time with the effort at hand, so that we will be taking inventory of the capacities from which to choose, and assigning each to a task and, in this way, making a continuous series of creative inventions possible.

5. The builder's vocation stands out in all its fullness, all its solidarity, all its unity at a point midway between the activity of the architect and that of the engineer—between the absolute architect, at one extreme, and the absolute engineer, at the other, two extremes which in fact meet in meditation of the most exalted type. *And so it is that the works of human builders express unity—a unity comparable to that which nature itself achieves in its own constructions.*

In ancient times and up until more recent eras, before the violent intrusion of applied mathematics and its consequences in the world of machines and their products, it had been possible for the builder to be *only one person,* possible for him to dominate a state of affairs which did not crush him by its multiplicity. The geometer of ancient times, the master builder in the Middle Ages, the architect in modern times supervised the use of simple techniques and solved simple problems. This is how certain great minds were able to elevate quality, along with imagination, to such a degree. They could take the whole responsibility on themselves. This is what the machine-age civilization changed.

Given this new situation in the history of building, the architect's vocation and the engineer's as well need to be defined so that through a judicious assignment of tasks, responsibility can recover its run-down virtue—that is, its indispensable power—and can be given to the person who should rightfully assume it in each sector.

A man can be made responsible only for what he knows.

The question of preparing people to assume their RESPONSIBILI-TIES brings up the entire problem of training people to build.

Definition of the teaching to be given:

. . . .
. . . .
. . . .

Even less than ever before are we dealing in preconceived ideas— of the academic variety or the futuristic cogitation variety. We are concerned with the difference between "preconceived ideas" and the sound inventions which are possible today and which are applicable in Rouen, for instance, or at Le Havre, Lorient, Dunkirk, Tours or Brest—all cities having been destroyed somewhat during the war; applicable too to Paris, a city which has become monstrous, and to Marseilles, plunged into disorder, and to Algiers, experiencing dangerous growing pains.

Technology, objectivity, grandeur and splendor can be the terms of one and the same equation. Everything that is technical and everything that is spiritual mobilized.

To loosen the stranglehold on cities and bring in some joy of living there is talk of building (under certain conditions) apartment buildings 165 feet tall:

"Never! What's been done in America urges against it . . ."

Alas! The people who say that don't have any information either on America or on the problem involved here.

For that matter, could it be that France is afraid of heights?

Notre Dame dominated the Ile-de-France region, rising above the pointed roofs of Gothic houses. Louis XIV made the mass of the Val-de-Grâce jut up straight from the bareness of the plateau de Saint-Jacques.

Another thing: war has razed the centers of cities—Orléans, Tours, Beauvais, Rouen, etc. Only the churches and the cathedrals are still standing. The overall pattern can be symbolized like this:

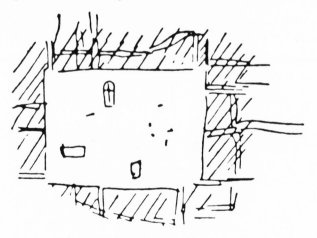

That being the case, what needs to be done? To arrange things in such a way as to place these cities squarely amidst present-day living conditions; that is:

They are points of passage; large numbers of people are in transit in these cities, but they are also points of culmination (on the one hand, transit; on the other, focussing and scattering).

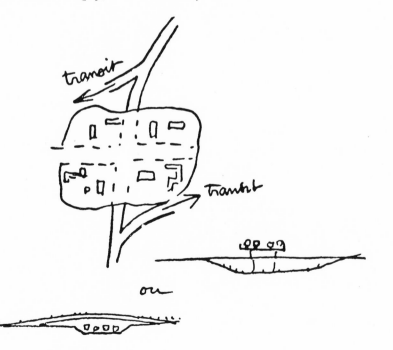

Next, to create a destiny for the center of the city, the center that has been razed and so is empty, and therefore *free*.

In this central portion, and with careful attention to the apportionment of the great amounts of space needed at ground level for circulation, erect the few high-density buildings that are essential to the vitality of the city: the business center, the guildhall, surrounded by the forum. . . . Make this center a sort of reserve kept at the disposition of future essential urban bodies.

Make advantageous use of the free space on the ground; *preserve* the space that is free; *magnify* things by the feeling of space.

Raise up into the sky, in the midst of space (azure and greenery), a few buildings that we will consider, a priori, handsome and worthy, proof of optimism, of a capacity for technology and sensitivity. In Rouen, this emptiness will place the outstanding beauty of the cathedral in a setting whose splendor one must know how to discover and recognize.

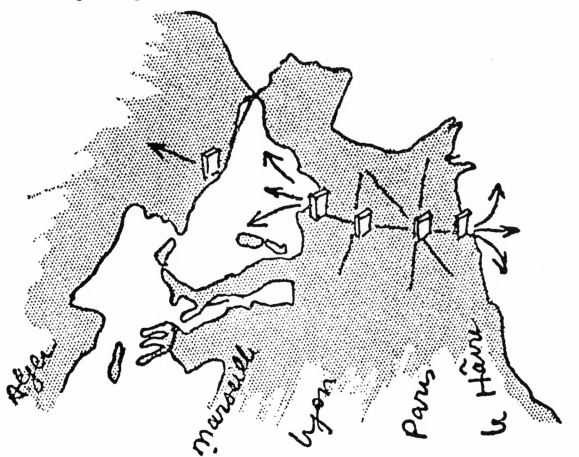

Greenery will occupy the emptiness left by demolition; the dwellings (and grocers follow the dwellings, not the church!) will be on the other side of the water.

In Orléans, an architectural composition of outstanding plastic quality will demonstrate reconquered dignity, the spirit of grandeur, the blood flowing once again in the country's veins. This will dazzle ourselves and foreigners too. Tradition will have been revived.

What all this means is that in this age of steel, glass, reinforced cement, there is a certain possibility of incorporating a certain number of exalted architectural feats into these predestined sites. Such architectural feats express the life of the cities and of the countries, as did, in the old days, the "grand'places" with their guildhalls and their town halls. Situated along a line of significance, a meridian of stimulus, Le Havre, Paris, Lyons, Marseilles have to have business cities, administra-

tive centers in order to fulfill an undeniable function—that of trade—
to the best of their abilities. These four cities, these four magnificent
milestones are certainly not going to make the country ugly. No! We are
not talking about preconceived ideas on ugliness or beauty.

No, we are not talking about preconceived ideas in this book. . . .

There is no denying that a certainty, an acquired thought, a new
practice, a new attitude taken once discoveries have been put to use—
these are not the fruit of invention alone. Discussion also plays a prime
role—discussion that can just as easily be on a friendly tone as on one
of villainy or foul play. What difference does it make! That's the way an
idea takes root in the midst of life, just as, in a landscape, a plant or a
tree will take root and its germination and its upward thrust will depend
on the virtue or the quality of the seed and also on the virtue or the
quality of the piece of land.

Architectural heights on the land of France, four landmarks of French
greatness pointing to a destiny of cities that has already been forged by

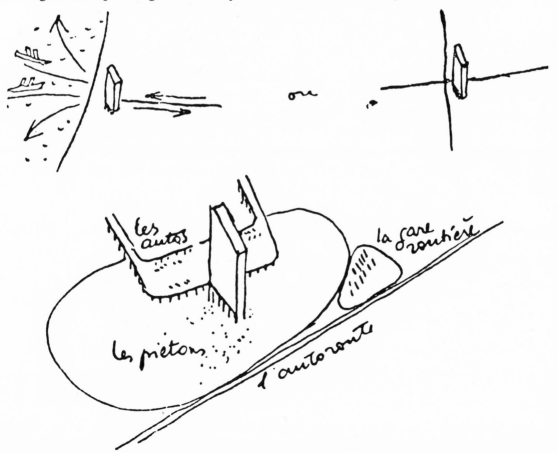

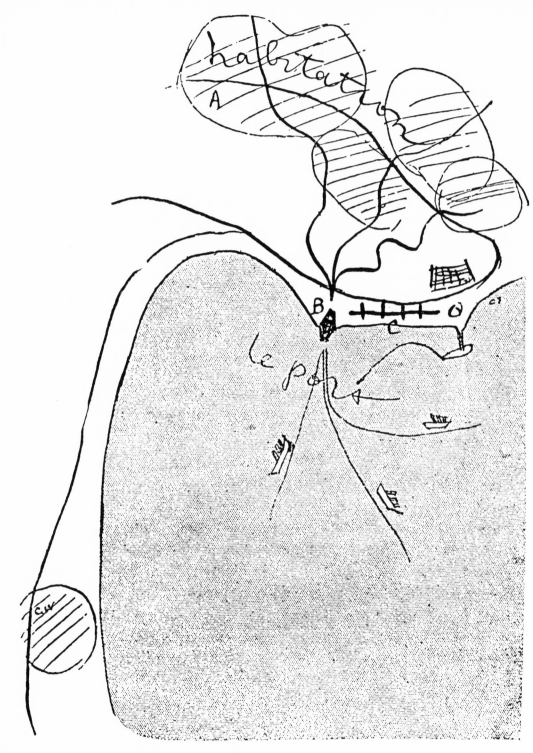

history and pinpointed by geography. And which, this time, express the history and the geography . . . that *have yet to come.*

To the west, Nantes . . .

If France feels it has a duty to offer its idea here, its conclusion, that is not because it has too lofty an opinion of its inventors; they are not worth any more or any less than those of other countries. But France itself constitutes a very special sort of soil, extraordinarily fertile, filled with human resonances. In the same way, it is this same soil which nurtures its wines and which, transposed to the spiritual level, will nurture its thought. It is this soil which makes the things on it human.

Now, this remark mustn't be allowed to flatter the braggarts, the sluggards, the complacent. Whereas the portrait of France, in the album of the world, may show a frivolous and impulsive exterior, its achievements, like the achievements of its great men, are terribly distinct, firm and concise, with precise edges and contours. No negligence, no niggling; instead, accuracy and categorical determination. Facts in the pure state.

Cartesian spirit, nature and man together in oneness and understanding, and not the *artificial* position of a society outside of nature.

The sketch showing Algiers, showing the planned development of a city which, on the threshold of a new Africa, brings together the history of two civilizations, difficult topography redeemed by the most beautiful landscapes, geography embracing two continents, a prodigious future— that sketch reveals firmness due to clear principles, and at the same time, diversity and adaptability, products of a happy marriage between men and nature, between day-to-day reality and lofty intention. The administrator, the architect-city-planner, the engineer hold in their hands the destiny of a city fated to preside over the destiny of a country.

CHAPTER 10
Applications and plans

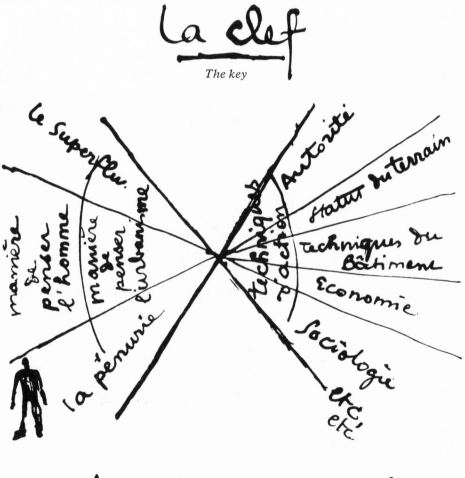

La **clef**

The key

L' urbanisme est une Clef

City planning is a key

General principles

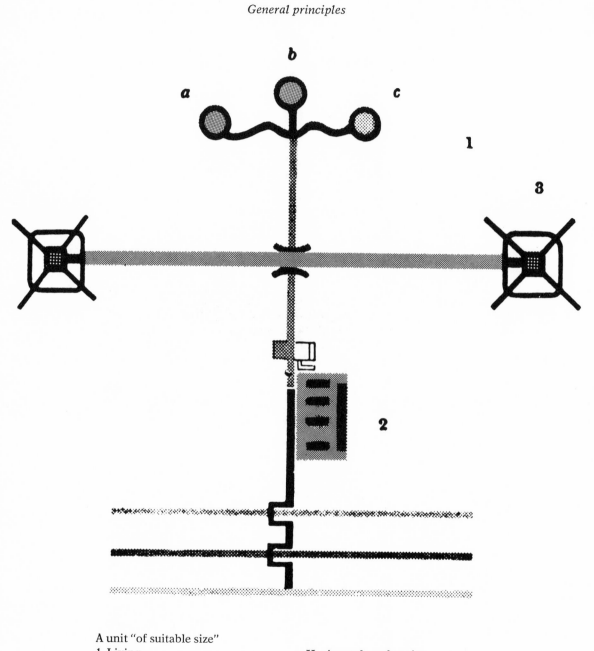

A unit "of suitable size"
1 Living
2 Working
3 Cultivating oneself

a Horizontal garden city
b Vertical garden city
c The extensions of the dwelling

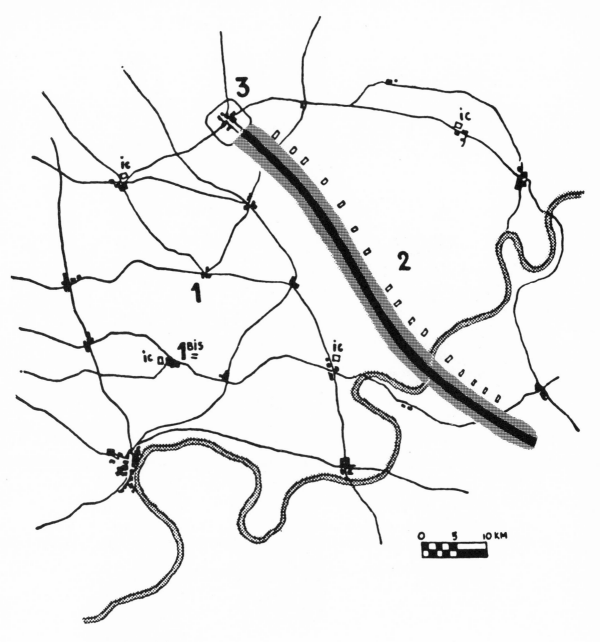

Natural conditions

1 The great land reserve
2 The linear industrial city
3 The radio-concentric trading city

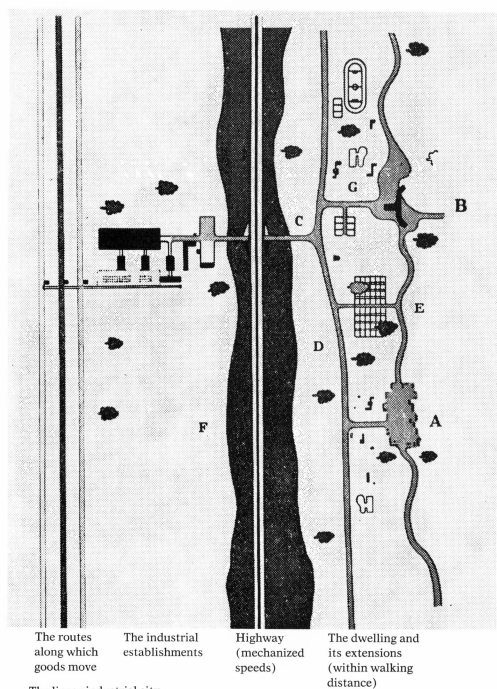

The routes along which goods move

The industrial establishments

Highway (mechanized speeds)

The dwelling and its extensions (within walking distance)

The linear industrial city

Caption for illustration on facing page

A The family dwelling in the form of little houses scattered in a horizontal garden city.

B The family dwelling in the form of little houses gathered together and placed on top of one another in a unit built all at the same time, a sort of vertical garden city.

C The crosswise access road to the factory.

D The road leading off to the dwellings and their communal services (can be used by cars).

E The connecting road and promenade (no cars allowed).

F The green zone of protection separating residential area from factory (and including the longitudinal highway of the linear city).

G The area set aside for communal services outside the dwelling: nursery school, primary schools, movies, libraries, all the sports facilities for everyday use (soccer, tennis, walking, racing, swimming, etc.), children's playground, teenagers' clubs, etc., small private gardens (to which individuals are entitled on request), garden plots for flowers, fruit or vegetables.

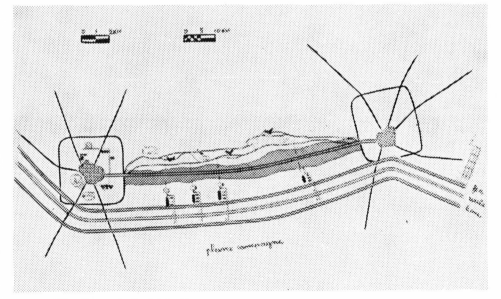

The linear industrial city.

In order to make the synthesis of this drawing possible, we have made it show, on three different scales, the industrial city, the radio-concentric city, the pattern of the three routes.

City planning of Algiers

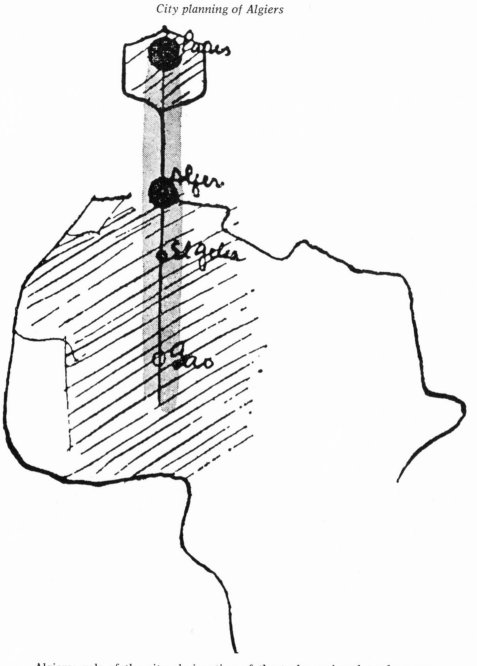

Algiers: role of the city, designation of the tasks assigned to the population, wise limitation warding off invasion by parasitical activities.

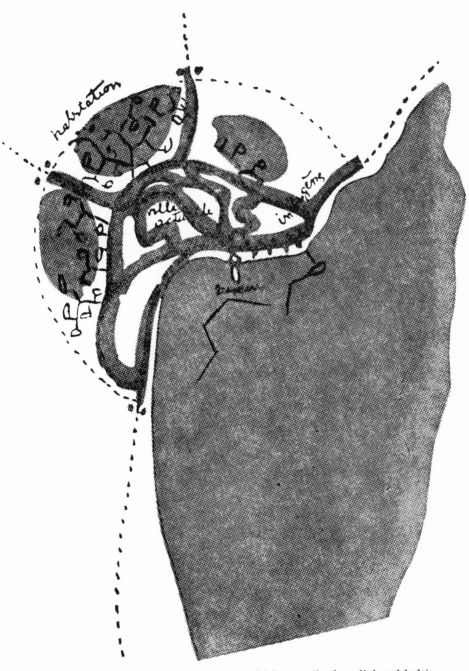

City boundaries and landmarks: master highways (both radial and belt);
channelling of circulation into the business center; irrigation of the future
civic center; rational passageway through the Quartier de la Marine.

le dedans

le dehors

The inside

The outside

Recognition of the constituent elements of the natural setting. Specific measures for protection and reconstitution. The city planning of the Arabs is excellent.

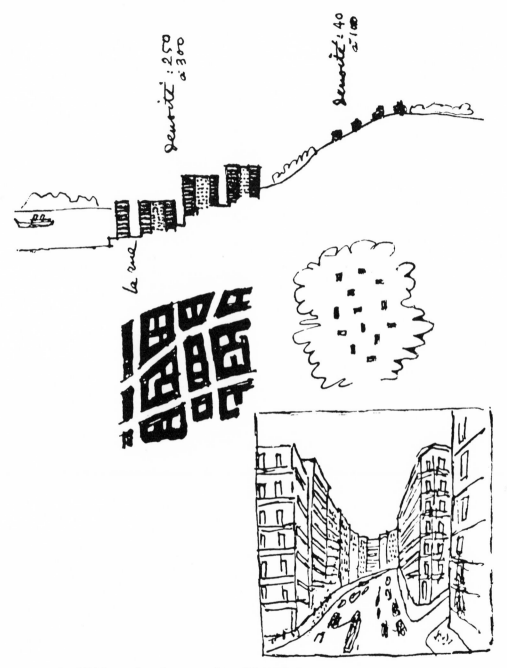

Prohibitions placed on two harmful customs:
   a) the block of houses built on streets and courtyards;
   b) allotment of real estate.
European city planning is harmful.

123

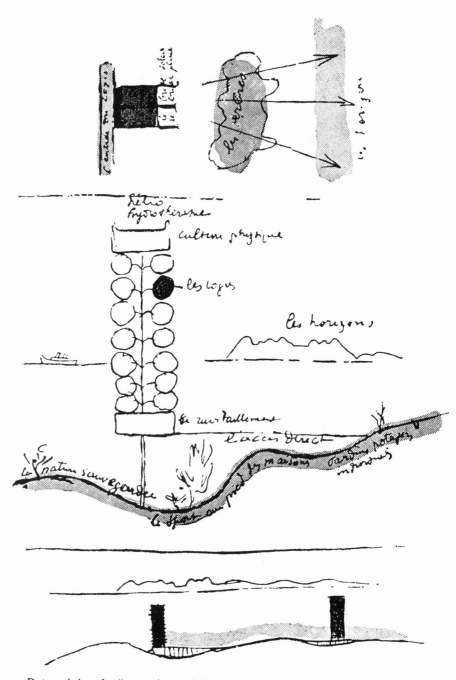

Determining the "extensions of the dwelling" that proceed from the housing unit (designating the organs whose necessity has been acknowledged): day nurseries, nursery schools, primary schools, youth centers, sports for children, adolescents, adults, individual garden plots.

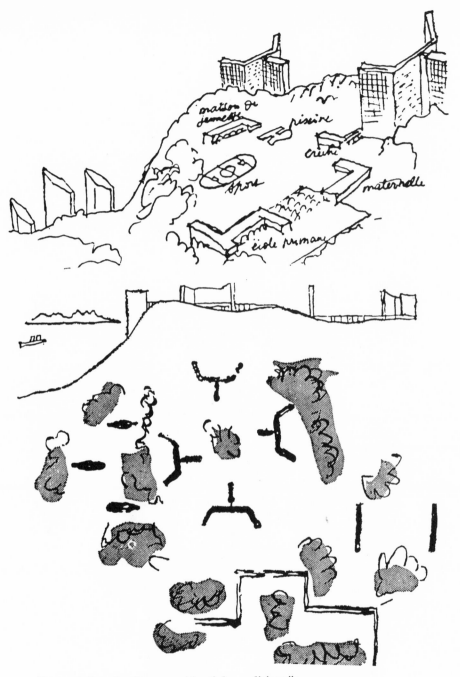

Determining the "new residential conditions":
    a) compulsory per-square-mile density;
    b) ratio of built-on area to area left free;
    c) new forms of the "constructed volume".

125

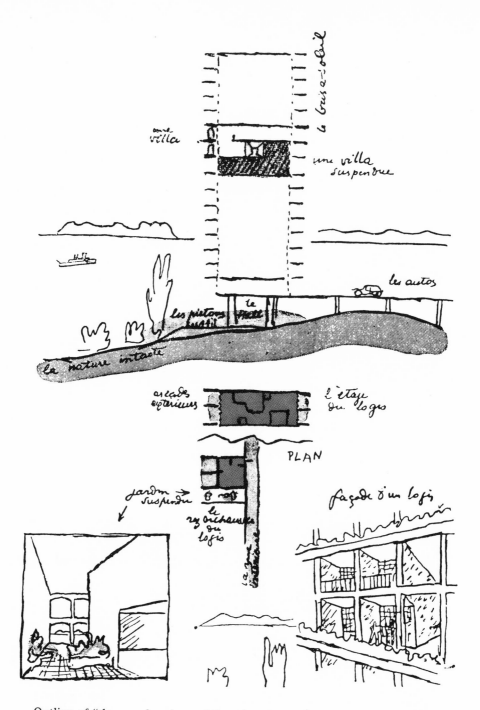

Outline of "the new housing unit" equipped with its integral or adjacent facilities.

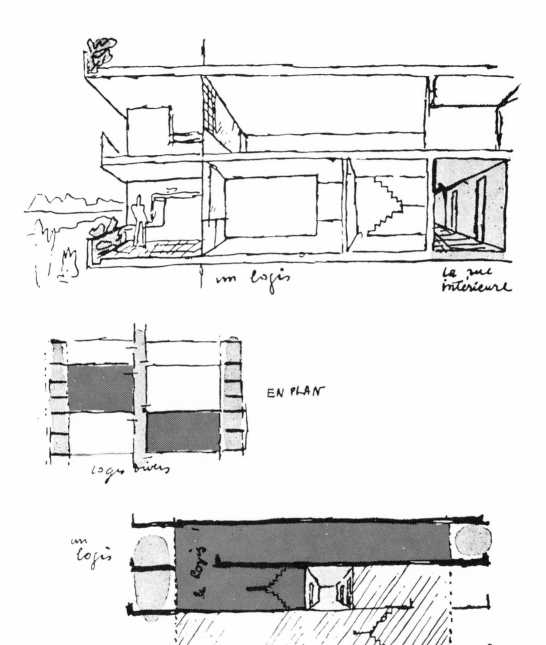

Creating new municipal housing regulations, bringing the home into harmony with the conditions obtaining in North Africa (height of the dwelling: 4.5 meters, subdivisible into twice 2.2 meters, etc.).

127

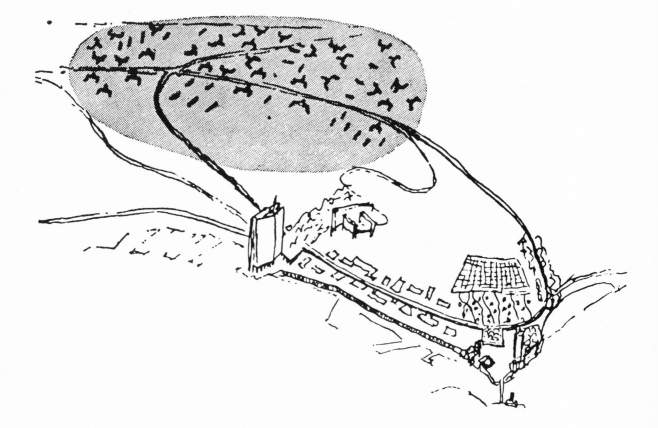

The land acquires a statute:

residential zone, business district, future civic center, the Casbah spared, creation of the Moslem cultural center.

Urban Development of Paris (Voisin Plan, 1925)

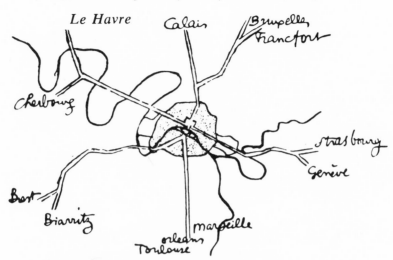

Paris: a large-scale operation is urgently needed.

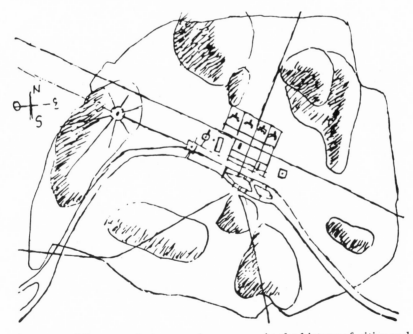

The automobile, an entirely new phenomenon in the history of cities and a thoroughly disturbing one, necessitates adequate adjustments:
    a) opening up an east-west throughway;
    b) opening up a throughway to the north.

Paris has transformed itself where it stood, on its own ground, without fleeing. Each new current of ideas, over the centuries, has been incorporated into its stones. This is how the living face of Paris has been formed. Let Paris continue.

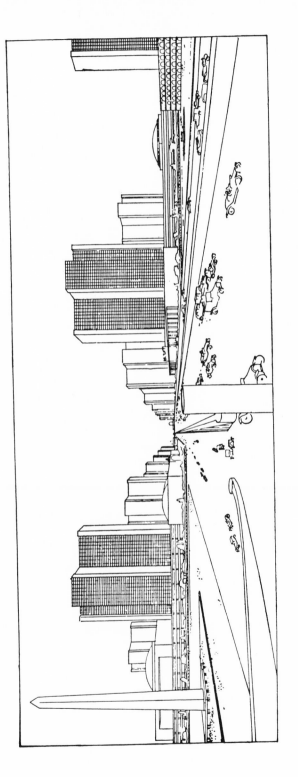

A contemporary city: the "urban phenomenon" seen from the throughway that crosses the city. To the left and right, the public service plazas. Farther back, the museums and universities. The whole figure formed by the skyscrapers is seen here bathed in light and air.

Standing out from this plain creased with insignificant constructions that stretches toward Saint-Denis, far from the
witnesses gathered along the banks of the river, four major
architectural events will occupy an extensive amount of space,
to the glory of a civilization which, instead of abdicating, will
have laid down a new line of conduct for itself.

Overall view of the scale model of the "Voisin Plan."

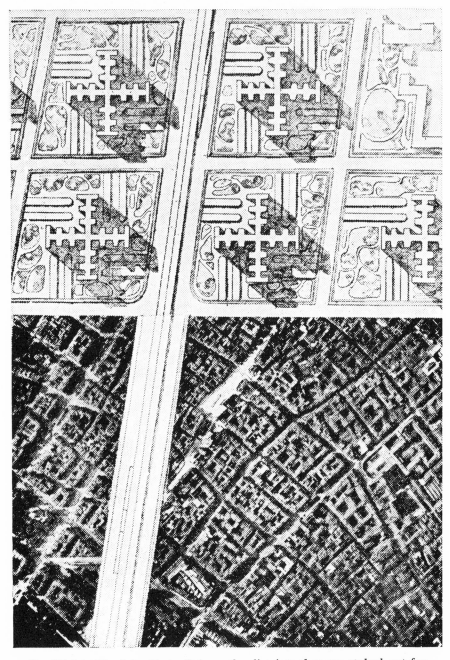

The "Voisin Plan" for Paris. Below: the districts that are staked out for demolition. Above: the districts with which it is proposed to replace them. (Both these plans are on the same scale.)

appendices

APPENDIX I
Statement by Ascoral

ASCORAL is an association of builders for an architectural renewal. Its goals are:

—to examine the way in which the ground is occupied especially by buildings and the extensions thereof: circulation and space left free;

—to arrive at a coherent doctrine of building and its extensions, the benefits of which could be extended to the entire country—cities and rural areas—and which correspond to the four functions: living, working, cultivating mind and body, getting about;

—to make the doctrine widely known;

—to persuade the authorities to adopt it;

—to see that it is put into practice throughout the country.

This association does not bring together professional practitioners of a single discipline (architecture) only, but in fact is open to all disciplines that are more or less closely connected with that of building: sociologists, architects, engineers, thinkers, teachers, scientists, peasants, workers, leaders, economists, legal experts.

An association without any preconceived limits, growing naturally by co-optation. Laying down, through the joint efforts of its members, an ARCHITECTURE and CITY-PLANNING doctrine. In the midst of the grab-bag conditions and the chaos of unprepared attempts to get the nation's engine started, it decides to offer a certainty: the clear-eyed vision, expressed without fear of criticism, of a destiny which a machine-age civilization offers to this country (and all other countries, too). Destiny manifest in *all that is built*—in fact, the toolkit of a society which today is capable of fostering the harmonious accomplishment of the most legitimate gestures. The substance which awaits discovery in the material and spiritual factors constituting our civilization will be laid bare, analyzed, explained, clarified by words and images, rid of anything that may be obscure about it—on the contrary, courageously held up in the unambiguous light for all to see, for the country to judge.

The country is faced with an ineluctable task: that of adjusting what it builds to the realities of a machine-governed civilization; conscience is involved as clearly as are the acts of the material life. The reconstruction projects necessitated by the war would form an enormous program in themselves, but they must not screen or camouflage the total mission which has devolved upon the immediate heirs of the upsets the world is experiencing today.

People are of two minds, and those minds are plunged into confusion. Some of them yearn for a bygone age, *moeurs* or setting, because they cling to the hope that there they will find security and happiness once again. The others measure the artificiality of going into reverse gear that way and believe that by looking ahead of them they will find virgin soil that will lend itself to the natural and harmonious development of events.

Preceding societies were of a pre-machine-age type. Today's society is a machine-age society. Radical and upsetting transformation. Ruins of an outdated civilization everywhere.

A prodigious reality: the power of machines bringing abundance and the very means needed to distribute it.

Retreat into the past or acceptance of the natural process of things—a choice has to be made between the one or the other.

Seen in a worldwide perspective, France—the only country to have lived an extraordinary sequence of two millennia without an eclipse—has the potential to discover ways and means of offering the spirit, despite contradictions and confusion, the assurance of its clarity of interpretation, its freedom of invention, its power of decision, its means of construction. France has a duty to contribute to the realm of building, within the machine-age civilization, the security that lies in sound and harmonious concepts.

Plans will be drawn for the construction of buildings (dwellings, farms, mills, places of relaxation or elevation of the mind), for the equipment of ports, for airlines, for the installation of traffic arteries within the population centers and for linking them with one another. The fate of the peasant or the worker must be taken care of—that aspect of it which is closest to the daily realities of his life, which makes for his happiness or his unhappiness: namely, his shelter, the shelter that either molests home and family or the shelter genuinely synonymous with joy. The steps that need taking in order to endow that shelter with all it must have cannot be mediocre, limited ones; what needs to be reconsidered is the way the very territory of the country is occupied, so as to ensure favorable surroundings both for the man who is guided by the annual rhythm of the sun—the peasant—and for the man who is merely organized by the day-to-day rhythm of the sun—the industrial worker.

The problem needing solution exceeds the simple technique of the art of building. What needs doing is to act as scout, as herald, bearing an element of decision: the true point of view.

A *true point of view* releases the harmony of productive acts; the law establishing its new articles, the cities, the towns, the farms and the land will call it to witness; the blueprints will be guided by this new outlook. And the public will bring the plan to life.

Everything is available; all the forces are there, ready: the machines, the means of transportation, the industrial organization, the administration, the pure science and the applied science. All of it preexists. The job is to wrest modern society from incoherence and guide it toward harmony. The world needs harmony, and it needs to be guided by harmonizers.

The mind must discern and the consciousness must designate the real goals of a society which has sunk into confusion at this time and which must be reunited—no more and no less—with its joy of living. A subjective postulate; the only one able to light the road ahead and determine the true program. The measure of efficiency will be the *human* element. Once that is so, then it will be possible to go ahead and plan . . . "The vicissitudes of peoples and the failures of human conceptions are in fact no more than the reaction of Nature intended to oblige the human mind to respect the universal order."

Gradually, and then all of a sudden violently, with the advent of machines, man was torn away from natural conditions . . . Today he is paying for it, realizing that he has let himself be submerged by massive disorganization. What must be done is to *reinstate natural conditions* and restore man to his veritable environment.

"There is oneness in the works of Nature and the works of the human mind." (Descartes)

"Recognizing the sovereignty of Nature, Descartes put an end to that of Reason, an end to the primacy of the word. It is no longer words which count, but realities."

139

APPENDIX II

The doctrine once laid down, how to apply it?

If we agree that an a priori doctrine can be established, we still face the question, how will it be put to use? Such a doctrine is made up of two objects. The first object concerns space, and that is the material nature of the programs which, through the efforts of the architect and the city planner, will install *imminent* facilities at various points on the surface of the country. Technology and spirituality—the two faces of human activity—will have led to the fructification which is sound evidence that a country has arrived at its own notion of happiness and, in so doing, has mapped out the programs for what it will produce and what it will undertake.

The second object concerns time, that is, the order in which measures are to be taken, each at its proper time. The chronology of operations, the meaning of the guidelines laid down by the plans and which must be instilled into the whole mass, so that order and efficiency will reign, rather than confusion and paralysis. A matter of authority, of government.

A question of professional aptitude and a question of attitude, each linked to the other. Only pioneers in laboratories are able, throughout a long period of time, to work out the outline of an experiment of capital importance. Sooner or later there comes a time when the outline has to be divulged, when the technicians have to be put to work, and everyone, depending on his capacity, made responsible for some useful part of the task, the users prepared to take up the new tools, the conductors of the experiment ready to see that it is carried out with sufficient regularity and intensity. Architects and engineers, users, jurists and administrators of the public domain—leaders, in short: these are the people for whom the doctrine is intended once it is established.

The ASCORAL doctrine must, by virtue of its rigorous postulates, obtain the approval of the technicians, architects and engineers who dispose of the necessary mental means of control: the present degree of technical perfection, the putting into use of materials available today, the tactical possibilities (in terms of time and of space) of what can be achieved, the conforming to the just and genuine aspirations of human nature—its needs and its duties, both individual and collective. These technicians will be won over to the doctrine. By "technicians" we mean, here, persons with sufficient knowledge and free of the passions unleashed by selfish or political considerations.

Technicians as such will find in the ASCORAL doctrine the most abundant materiality there is of the elements of modern city planning.

Whereas national reconstruction or equipment authorities today or private individuals (architects recently given the new title of city planner) are disturbed about the uncertainty felt at present over these grave problems, the doctrine will provide security and that sort of unanimity which does not rule out any of the multiple variants that enhance the mind and make life captivating and constantly renew it. This unanimity in a climate of security is the lever of sustained efforts all directed toward the oneness of purpose which is at the origin of great movements.

No such doctrine can stem from a single person alone. Those days are gone; one hundred and twenty revolutionary years have brought opportunities to advance hypotheses and to check them. Researchers' inventions have faced local judgment first, then, little by little, judgment on a universal scale, so that what was once an alarming proposal has become common practice everywhere. Thus the doctrine has, in fact, been sanctioned by a relative and adequate degree of unanimity, rallying many men who work in various disciplines all involved in fragmentary elements of the problem which one day, by the process of addition, became the program itself; unanimity which groups a specific quality of minds, whether modest or brilliant, but all free of conformism, that fruit of fear or cupidity. The doctrine has rallied temperaments situated on all rungs of the social ladder, minds busy in various fields of activity: workmen or businessmen, bourgeois or revolutionaries, the young or their elders, etc., sociologists, manufacturers, public or private administrators, doctors, architects and engineers, scholars, jurists, etc. It has brought together people who until then had been isolated in the convictions they had acquired in the course of ten or twenty or thirty years of personal labor; and to them it adds the action of the younger people, whose unshakeable faith is the outcome of an option.

This grouping of people, which represents two decades of what had been scattered and are now joint efforts, did not become active until just recently. Since its capacity is unlimited, it simply keeps growing in step with the investigation itself.

The substance of the doctrine will become available when published in several volumes. As objective as possible and undeniably general, although it will be the sum total of even minor analyses and inventions, it will touch the user. And the user will understand not only what the rights of a machine-age society are after the first century-long cycle of trial and error, but also what its duties are to the solidarity in which the social whole is enveloped.

Thus informed, the people responsible for administering the public domain will evaluate the extent of their obligations. Face to face with clearly expressed views on the part of their leaders and of those who form their own clientele, the persons who are to put the plan into effect will stop falling back on their defense positions. On the contrary, with the strength of their several talents massed behind them, they will approach this new work site that awaits them and offers them the finest opportunities to place their art and their passion at the service of the general good.

The ASCORAL doctrine is the outcome of work by eleven groups or subgroups. The motivation for setting up those groups was the wish to bring these questions out into the open as naturally and as spontaneously as possible; never, at any point, was it a pipe dream about compiling an encyclopedia of building. The aim is to provide the country, *at the appropriate time* and in an immediately assimilable form, with a degree of certainty which will be capable of orienting plans, undertakings and laws, without delay, and of inducing builders, jurists and leaders to venture onto the road toward creativity. Flaws there may be in the ASCORAL doctrine; but the idea is to fling open the doors and windows, let the technicians, the users and the leaders—the marrow of the country—unite in a single, sound intention as they face in the direction being taken by modern events, rather than facing backwards. The experience of modern industry has shown us that once all concerned actually bend to the task, then instant and miraculous elements of progress add up every day without exception, and in only a few years they reach a goal which centuries would never have been able to attain otherwise.

Next, study teams were formed, each of which was to formulate one practical proposal ready to be carried out, to the credit of building. The subsequent job of putting this into words would be done in books, which, together, would constitute the ASCORAL doctrine.

As the product of a prospecting effort made within present-day society, the doctrine is prepared to report on its conclusions.

Eight teams set to work.

TEAM   I: General ideas and synthesis.
TEAM   II: Notion: "knowing how to inhabit," at school.
TEAM   III: Standardization in building
        a) Subgroup on household equipment
        b) Subgroup on building dwellings
        c) Subgroup on industrializing dwellings.
TEAM   IV: Health.
TEAM   V: Work
        a) Subgroup on agriculture
        b) Subgroup on industry.
TEAM   VI: Folklore.
TEAM   VII: Financing and legislation.
TEAM VIII: Contracting

The entire undertaking is focussed on the dwelling considered as "central to the concern with city planning." It leaves a whole mass of questions untouched; they belong to the same stream and they will capture the attention of countless ingenious spirits who will spontaneously discover, for themselves, the paths that lead to the overall focal point.

TEAM I

General ideas and syntheses are an opportunity to discern the major constituent elements of the problem, to arrange them in a hierarchical pattern, and outline the climate for action—human on the one hand, natural on the other. And once this is done, to take a look at the country and at the other countries beyond it, draw the main blueprints, state the problem in so many words. Lastly, to unify to some extent the huge undertaking which building is: unity of places, times and techniques.

TEAM II

But the results achieved by that first team open up so much territory ahead of them that there could be room for impatience. The doctrine needs to know what direction to take; and once it starts on its way, the road leading to possible achievement will be long. The task is being undertaken and the first stage being gone through for the benefit of the new generations. A twenty-year grace period is not too much to allow the conceivers of plans. But right now, today, those who will be adults at the end of those twenty years must be acknowledged as potential users of buildings. What needs to be built is not intended as a sort of old-age home for anyone who might go on living on sterile sacrifice and uselessly hard work; the idea is, instead, to equip a society that needs to be set right and has a taste for the joy of living.

Preparation for this begins in elementary school and continues in high school. It is in the schools, with children who are at an age where they assimilate easily, that the material and spiritual viewpoints of the person who is to use a building should be revealed. Then the child or the youth, as he sits at the family table or takes part in teen-age groups, will bring the issue before his elders—evidence of the awareness of duty in the rising generation, faced with the virtualities of the times.

TEAM III

Obviously, it will take some time before things will really get under way. Man's dwelling—the dwelling itself and the extensions of it—is a gigantic theme, needing much exploration.

a) First of all, stating the problem in so many words: how to equip the dwelling. This goes straight to the heart of the doctrine, with its repercussions: a necessary and adequate dwelling is to be defined and will constitute the number one problem of modern manufacturing. Equipment of the dwelling considered as the prime element in the equipment of the country; consequently, accounting for the biggest or heaviest portion of its manufacturing programs and necessarily calling upon its utmost production resources: its industry.

b) The subgroup on construction will be looking for two sorts of elements and so paving the way for industrialization: first of all, the dimensions that are determined by human gestures and will in turn determine the height of the premises to be built, the amount of area they cover on the ground, the proportion of household installations, their location in relation to one another, their contiguities. In short, the actual biology of the dwelling. Secondly, the measures that must be taken in terms of the strength of materials, the application of industrial methods to their use, in the name of economy; the determination by these factors of the spacing between posts, the length of beams, the systems to be used for soundproofing, insulating, etc.

c) Only at that point can industrialization in both forms be envisaged: the production (fabrication) of a sequence of standardized elements, or mass production of standardized dwellings.

TEAM IV

Checkup by a doctor or, better yet, forecast by the health officer, who will have had first say. The ASCORAL point of view will be reasserted: bring to present-day society the joy of living to which it is entitled. Health comes before everything else; and between physical and moral health there are close ties, an intimate psychophysiological relationship, living conditions and environmental conditions. Basic rules of hygiene to be complied with in the home just as in the workshop or the office. The need to denounce the agents that are hostile to fulfillment of one's being, to state the terms of corporal discipline, to make the advice or the urgings of doctors, hygiene specialists and biologists widely known.

TEAM V

The doctors will have pointed out the threat that looms over a society having cut itself off little by little from natural conditions. The dwelling is not all that is involved; most of a lifetime, after all, is spent at one's work. Not only must the office, the workshop, the factory be so arranged as to comply with the doctor's orders but also the very behavior of men in relation to their machines must be reexamined.

Everything must be weighed all over again—the raison d'être of today's cities, their frenzied accumulations and dangerous mixtures; the reasons for the exodus from the rural areas. The two major branches of work, agriculture and industry, oblige us to reconsider the way the ground itself is occupied—

the way men have scattered themselves over the land or have taken it over, as they have covered it, little by little, with cities, industrial centers, villages and farms. As the machine-age civilization installed itself, it improvised, above all. Things being left to private initiative, the results were arbitrary working, housing and transportation conditions, the degradation of the landscape and of souls, leading to a state of affairs which is contrary to the welfare of the species.

Work, that natural human activity, has become a sinister thing in many cases, an instrument of torture. If we agree that joie de vivre is the culmination of the reforms that are desired, then work in pleasant conditions is the very instrument by which to achieve it. At a time when joy seems to be relegated to the opposite pole from that of work, it is worthwhile to indicate, specifically, what material arrangements should be made so that work will recover its dignity: determination of efficient industrial zones and the facilities to be set up in them; valid forms of administrative work; rural adjustments intended to renovate peasant life.

TEAM VI

The decision to take charge of the country's surface once again naturally leads to taking inventory of what is to be found on that surface: places, sites, and man-made structures. We can draw up a balance sheet with, on the credit side, the natural treasures and the human creations worthy of transmitting their message to us and, on the debit side, the false maneuvers that have sullied the landscape and rushed to put up buildings any old way. The balance sheet reveals a source of capital from which it might be helpful and possible to derive some wealth; by this is meant the spiritual value with which many and many a human undertaking is imbued, and which is labelled, folklore, the flower of tradition. Man, as a product of the universe, embodies the very rules of the cosmos, and whenever he has acted on the stimulus of favorable influences, he has been able to express them spontaneously and thereby create harmony. A type of harmony which we perceive as an agreement with the universe, the profound and intimate satisfaction of oneness, basis of poetic events eminently suited to delight us. The poetry and tradition inscribed in human achievements can be effaced as a consequence of our negligence. What is worthy of being preserved, classified, inventoried, placed in the common fund of a society's didactic equipment should be pointed out as such. But to carry things further still, can the poetic values of traditions that have disappeared or that may still be vivid be used as genuine models in structures of the times: or will they merely be lessons? And further still: would we be entitled, in the context of our imminent undertakings, to look for and designate factors capable of becoming supporting elements for created things which may one day have the honor of being included in the "folklore" category?

In a word, can we find among the existing things with recognized folklore value, laws or even rules which would be more or less applicable to our forthcoming efforts in the field of building?

TEAM VII

A great program for equipping the machine-age civilization has been formulated; the upcoming generations are preparing for it; everything having to do with building is being standardized, salvaged from incoherence, and action in every area is regulated by the supervision of biologists, doctors, hygiene specialists;—agriculture and industry raise the question of how the surface of the country is to be occupied; stock is taken of folklore-type values which might be useful; there remains to find out which legal and financial measures will be able to make room in life for all things. First of all the plan was outlined, its end purpose being joy of living for a society wed by fate to its machines. This plan is a monument of contemporary activity; it is not futuristic; it is present. It indicates the volume of our undertakings, constitutes the legitimate program for our manufacturing efforts; and where the building is to be done in the country, it tries to bring big industry into the picture, assigning a beneficial purpose to the gigantic quantity of energy which has been absorbed so far in evil-doing (producing cannon). The *plan* will force modern society to face the facts by spelling out its reasons for living and the goals of its activity throughout the duration of an initial cycle: the cycle of harmony of the machine-age civilization.

Legal steps will need to be taken to release land and money—actually, shattering some of the age-old constraints that no longer have tenure in this age of machines.

This is where the wager is being laid; inventory of the available means is taken; the programs are mapped out that will be needed and are adequate to bring into equilibrium a society which a hundred years of mechanization are projecting into an adventurous future. If we don't act, wars will result, both within and between countries. If we decide to act, steps can be taken that will have serious consequences. The choice is open: action or inaction.

From then on, all we will have to do is—do, undertake. The doers, the contractors have the floor. Inventory of the means available, timetable of the stages to be gone through. There's a battle to be waged; more, in fact: a war to be won. It calls for a combination of strategy and tactics.

The inventory for this country shows a categorical ratio between one-man operations of the artisan type and big firms. But the plan itself includes a characteristic pattern of distribution of jobs suited to local artisans and large-scale enterprises which can be taken on only by large groups of firms.

No such overall view has yet been given the country by its services, its specialists or its poets. No governmental or municipal organization could attempt this grand approach.

Putting its roots deep down into the most varied disciplines, ASCORAL has assigned itself this task. It has dared to envisage the ultimate aim, which is an ethical whole defining the spiritual current of the undertaking. Through its technicians, ASCORAL knows that all of the solutions envisaged are accessible, and this gives it the right to express itself and faith in the value of what it proposes.

APPENDIX III

Eleven study groups drew it up

TEAM I

GENERAL IDEAS AND SYNTHESIS

A resolutely and definitively technical world reveals unexpected, unknown and unlimited spaces to the mind. The dream flings open wide its doors. Technique and spirituality are quite precisely interdependent. A way of thinking suited to the aptitudes of the times foments a new state of consciousness, and that consciousness, nourished on the vital currents of our day, will quite naturally erect its buildings, receptacle and shelter for men, for things and for thoughts. And in this way the age of renovation has already begun.

Now, the architectural revolution had been accomplished one hundred years before.

It is worthwhile recognizing and obeying the rule that will constitute the measuring instrument according to which, in the last analysis, all questions will be judged and settled. The yardstick is not money, which sprawled all over this century of the greatest effort and has dirtied everything. Nor will it be mechanical efficiency. The yardstick is a thoroughly subjective one, and ASCORAL chose it in order to shed the light of reality on all of its proposals: the joy of living.

ASCORAL does not intend to produce a modern encyclopedia of building. A chimerical idea; the task would be unlimited and the product would be illusory, since whatever has to do with building in the machine-age civilization belongs to the future and will in fact represent the outstandingly important effort of modern society dominating its machines and disposing of unheard of quantities of energy in order to equip itself with the simple, natural and possibly magnificent set of tools which will make its undertakings fruitful and beneficial: suitable shelters.

No, ASCORAL's general ideas, as expressed here, will instead prop up, so to speak, a way of reasoning—a frank and disinterested manifestation of a point of view: life, environment, technology . . . A factual demonstration of the law of harmony to which one can feel entitled to attach that subtle and immaterial thing of an outstandingly sensitive nature which is called happiness.

A development from cause to effects, a series of links from one undertaking to the next—these do not stem from discussions within coteries but from the very realities of life: society in full action, work on the land and in industry, rest at home, a home whose constituent realities are to be looked at clearly and firmly. ASCORAL is concerned about the dwelling and the extensions of it and believes that it can open up an era of active initiative to a society that has reached the end of its rope today, a society that is splintered with hatred. A hundred years ago mankind broke with the rate of speed it had always known—a walking pace of 3 miles per hour—and found itself endowed with mechanically-produced rates of speed: everything was placed in doubt. ASCORAL takes a new look at the very way in which the ground is occupied; and that way, which—fortunately—is guided by the exploitation of the opportunities inherent in mechanization, then brings the farm laborer and the factory worker into harmony.

We are not talking about preconceived ideas but about elements of a doctrine for which nine ASCORAL study teams are responsible, and which can be interpreted as a *declaration of the duties of man toward society* and—here we are thinking of France in particular—toward the nation.

Once the doctrine has been laid down, it will be used, brought before the public, before the technicians and the government.

Concomitant phenomena will then take place all over the country: events of plastic, ethical, aesthetic importance. Lyricism taking over a society and acting as its lever.

TEAM II

PEDAGOGY

This teaching task belongs to our generation.

One day, the children of today will constitute the generation that will be using the facilities we will have installed for it. This new social mass has to be prepared; it will be trained from earliest childhood on, in the schools.

The task of imparting the new lessons will be entrusted to teachers, both men and women, in the nursery schools, the elementary schools and the secondary schools. A specific notion needs to be made current throughout the country, the one that engenders material acts and also lights the lamps of sensitivity and thought.

Knowing how to inhabit a dwelling!

It has been found that in the midst of the overall refuse of our society-at-an-end, facilities everywhere are lacking or defective—the schools like all the rest (housing, places of work, places of recreation).

For instance, there are some 32,000 rural schools in existence. A great many of these are blighted by now and not to be stood for any longer. So the program calls for the construction of 32,000 school buildings with the appropriate equipment. The latter element is new, since in order to achieve social equilibrium one day, based on the notion of *knowing how to inhabit*, it will be necessary to draw up the programs and the teaching methods among which the topic of building will be included. Some 32,000 teaching laboratories must be built. Instead of palatial schools, flawless barracks.

The topic of building will be introduced into the teaching dispensed in the elementary schools and in the secondary schools.

And from there, what is taught at school will spread to the home. In discussions around the family table, the child will contribute the new life that is introduced by a judicious interpretation of the notion, *Knowing how to inhabit.* "Father and mother sleep all their lives; they tend to be asleep in every respect; it is essential that some new being shake them and prop them up with a fresh and vivid energy that no longer exists inside themselves. There must be someone who acts differently and who pops up every morning, saying, 'There is another life that you have forgotten. Learn to live better . . . !' " (MONTESSORI)

Study outline

Formulating qualitative programs and suitable sizes for:
—the dwelling,
—the extensions of the dwelling,
—the housing unit.

It is not this Team's responsibility to study the means which will ensure that these programs will be carried out. The *Construction and Industrialization* Team and the *Legal and Financial* Team will take care of that.

So the work of the *Household Equipment* Team will consist of:

Gathering all the data on the basis of which the problems involved in the "dwelling" function can be stated.

Giving those problems concrete expression.

Analyzing the various possible ways of solving them.

Drafting programs to be offered to builders and industrialists, once it is possible to do so to a sufficiently general degree.

A great many questions will come up in the course of the study, and they will not be given specific answers because they cannot be solved in the absolute.

It is just as well not to have any illusions on that score and not to lay claims to producing the definitive document on the "dwelling" function.

The idea is to outline a general study method, give examples of how it can be applied, lay down the rules that already seem essential—and so establish the concrete elements of a coherent doctrine that will be enhanced by each subsequent application of it.

The study will be made from the inside out—that is, starting from individual problems and aiming for collective solutions, and, in every instance, moving from an analysis of the needs involved to a definition of the means by which to satisfy them.

It will comprise the following stages:

—A general study of the basic needs of the different categories of people, considered as users of the housing unit.

Hence the definition of the various categories of problems to be solved.

—A critical study of the solutions usually adopted.

—The study as such of the facilities that are desired.

Each elementary problem on which there will be a detailed analysis of the needs to be met will be pursued right up to a specific statement of the goal to be achieved by the desired facilities which will provide a basis for the research done by the other technical teams.

The various likely solutions will be criticized on the basis of their effectiveness only—that is, the quality of the services rendered by each of them.

The following summary was prepared so that a work scheme could be established and tasks distributed among the various members of the Team and also so as to serve as the initial skeleton outline for the publication planned upon completion of the study.

Proposed summary, Part I

The basic needs.

The problems to be solved.

Preliminary note. Definition of the categories of users who will be considered, according to:

> their resources,
> their age,
> their tastes,
> the number of them in a single family.

A. Physiological needs.

Problems —Protection. $\left\{\begin{array}{l}\text{weather}\\\text{temperature}\\\text{noise}\end{array}\right.$

> —Ventilation.
> —Light.
> —Sleep.
> —Food.
> —Hygiene.

B. Material needs.

 Problems —Maintenance. $\left\{\begin{array}{l}\text{premises} \\ \text{clothing}\end{array}\right.$

    —Service.
    —Child care.
    —Circulation.
    —Budget.

C. Psychological needs.

Man demands of the setting of his day-to-day life something more than the mere satisfaction of his physiological and material needs.

What are the psychological needs that the builder must take into account— that is, the needs that will result in certain forms, dimensions, arrangements or a pattern of organization within the housing unit?

The psychological or material needs are undeniable facts; all it takes to define them is a logical mind. At this point in the study however, it will be necessary to bring into clear focus the concept of life in the dwelling which is to serve as a basis for all the related work: respect of the individual, reality of family life, social contacts of all types . . . all of these facts will influence the way dimensions are selected, space distributed, the extensions of the dwelling organized, etc. . . .

Some clear ideas on this infinitely sensitive topic must be got down on paper.

Problems
—of an aesthetic nature
   —indoor space,
   —walls,
   —views, terraces,
   —furniture,
   —buildings, proportions, dimensions,
   —gardens, arrangements, plantings,
   —circulation (patterns of movement).
—of life inside the dwelling
   —individual independence,
   —family equilibrium,
   —children's upbringing,
   —service,
   —friends.
—of life within the housing unit
   —family independence,
   —neighbors,
   —extensions of the dwelling.

Conclusion of Part One:
    —Deciding on the types of dwelling to be studied:
        individual volumes,
        interior arrangements,
        specification and quality of equipment,
        extensions of the dwelling.

Part Two

The present solutions. Criticism.

Could be shown usefully in synoptic tables indicating the materials and the classic arrangements used in response to the various needs previously analyzed; while critical comments on the value of the services rendered will reveal which facilities are especially poorly adapted, and it is on these that the study will bring its efforts chiefly to bear.

Similarly, a contrast will be clearly established between the needs satisfied by present facilities at a cost acceptable to all their users, and those which are satisfied only to a very minor extent or at a price which is generally out of reach or through outdated and socially intolerable processes.

Part Three
The rational solutions.

A.   The dwelling.

    —The functional spaces and their equipment.
        Room for sleeping.
        Washing-up room.
        Kitchen.
        Closets and cupboards.
    —The children's universe.
    —The home: A room for meditation and work.
        Dining room.
        Reception room or common room.
    —Plan of the recommended arrangements.
        Types.
    —Specifications of the well-defined elements entering into the construction of the dwelling.

B.   The extensions of the dwelling.

    —Collective bodies providing services that cannot be taken care of on the individual level.

—Separate study of each service, including:
    —Analysis of the needs to be satisfied.
    —Outline of possible solutions.
    —Determination of the optimum dimensions.
    —Study of the types of equipment to be planned.
    —Estimate of the necessary personnel.
    —Plan of the necessary premises.
    —Organizational, functional, administrative and financial outlines.
—Hotel service:
    —Reception, telephone, porter.
    —Upkeep of premises, of linen (washing . . .).

—Food:
    —Supply.
    —Preparation.
    —Service, tableware.
    —Possible restaurant.
    —Guest rooms.
    —Meeting rooms, music rooms . . .
    —Bar, billiards, games . . .
    —Independent studies or workrooms.
Garage. Possible do-it-yourself shop.
Health. Preventive medicine. Childbirth.
Infants' nursery. Kindergartens. School.
Sports. Playing fields. Games. Swimming pools.
Gardens. Farming.
Basic everyday shops and stores.

C.   Housing unit.

Size suited to needs and economically feasible.
Occupation of the ground:
        theoretical study;
        influence of construction costs;
        in the actual operational phase.

Dimensions and arrangements of the various elements.
Dimensions of buildings:
        shapes,
        height,
        thickness (depth from back to front),
        width.
Interior arrangements:
        dwelling,
        extensions,
        circulation (patterns of movement).

155

Arrangement on the ground:
> orientation,
> spacing.

Utilization of ground not built upon:

> circulation $\begin{cases} \text{vehicles} \\ \text{pedestrians} \end{cases}$

> gardens and sports.

Organization of the housing unit. Brief notes on:
> Property.
> Management.
> Staff.
> Services automatically provided.
> Services available on request.
> Budgets.

Conclusion:
> The various models planned.
> Model outlines.

TEAM III a.

HOUSEHOLD EQUIPMENT
WORK PROGRAM

Purpose of the study

To define the facilities needed to endow man's home with the most favorable atmosphere and ensure the satisfaction of its occupants' day-to-day physiological, material and psychological needs.

The (collective) housing unit is the category of building in which daily life takes place; it does not cover places of work or recreation nor cultural and administrative centers.

It is composed of a set of buildings and of free and planted spaces which include the dwellings and the extensions of them, as well as the necessary network for circulation.

Every resident of the "unit" can find everything he needs every day without going outside the "unit."

Horizontal distances are reduced to such an extent that no mechanized means of transportation is required within the territory of the "unit."

The housing unit is the basic component part of the city.

In the builder's way of thinking, the notion of the housing unit must replace that of the mere individual dwelling, which solves only a few housing problems.

Furthermore, in aesthetic terms, the housing unit contrasts with the principle on which today's cities were built—that of bit-by-bit construction based on the existence of the common (or "party") wall and the hideous consequences that that leads to.

It presupposes the possibility of regrouping building lots, without which no genuine city planning can be carried out.

Necessity of the study

Building activity at this time overlooks both:

—the concern with finding a rational way to satisfy the needs of all categories of users,

which leads to the moral or physical imbalance of their lives, of which they are more or less consciously aware;

—the means which recent techniques make available to it,

which leads to the paradoxical contrast between present industrial methods and contemporary conceptions of building, and to the major consequence of that paradox: the excessive cost of housing.

A whole segment of the population at this time is living in such dwellings and in such "districts" that it cannot have a proper perspective on the different human values.

If this state of affairs were to be altered, the consequences for the individual and for the whole of society would be tremendous.

Now, only through the rational use of present or possible techniques can this transformation be carried out in a way that is economically viable in the world such as it is today and which it would be vain to deny.

The various ASCORAL studies will bear out this statement.

For the sake of fully effective action, the technical means must be put to use in a coherent, purposeful way from the very beginning.

Accordingly, all housing problems must be foresightedly "thought through" all over again and rational solutions to them must be envisaged.

Which is the intention of the study being done by the *Equipment* Team.

TEAM III b.

CONSTRUCTION

This group's field of activity fits in between two distinct fields of knowledge:

Knowledge *of human needs;*
Knowledge *of the possibilities of materials.*

Construction must reconcile these needs with these possibilities.
Construction is the architect's answer, via the material means with which

engineers and industrials supply him, to the requests formulated by psycho-physiologists and hygiene specialists.

So we must draw up two lists: one of the *conditions imposed by Man*, and another, of the *conditions imposed by Materials*.

The study of the conditions imposed by human nature (on the individual level and on the social level) falls under the Health, Work, History and Human Geography Teams. These conditions are translated particularly by Team III a, *Household Equipment*, which is specifically concerned with the functions of the dwelling and its organic arrangements.

The study of the conditions imposed by materials lies within our province, but it also falls under Team III c, *Industrialization*, whose purpose is to reconcile the possibilities of a physical type with those of the economic type as defined by Teams VII, *Financing and Legislation*, and VIII, *Contracting*.

Of course we are not going to take a retrospective look at all the ways of building. We will simply recall that each of them was born out of a set of conditions characteristic of an era or a place. What matters to us is to group all those, whether ancient or recent, which are living today and which it is useful to employ, and to determine the *norms*.

Every norm represents an optimum that is valid for a certain time. While permanent as to its object, it is evolutive in its forms; for it is linked to progress in needs, in man's ambitions and in his means.

This optimum rarely coincides with an average, because it implies an improvement over the average. Sometimes the norm is a human minimum imposed on a material maximum; so it is with the norms governing the volume of the dwelling.

Man's ambitions are limited only by his imagination; in other words, they are not in themselves normative.

On the other hand, certain building norms depend on the form and dimensions of the human body and its movements; these are the *geometrical corporeal norms*.

Others depend to a greater extent on his organic functioning; these are the physiological norms, or *norms of atmosphere*.

At the opposite extreme, the Material used imposes its own limits and is sufficient in itself to define the optima or the norms.

These material norms will be *geometrical*—when expressed by special measurements—and *physical* when they depend on other qualities or are expressed by other measurable quantities.

Finally, *building norms*, as such, will stem from the synthesis of these basic norms. They will define the Complex Norms for the Construction of Dwellings, the dwelling being taken in its geometrical whole (gauges, for instance) or in some of its inner organs, whether localized (equipment units) or non-localized (circulatory systems).

And so this analysis leads to a practical classification, as follows, constituting our work program:

I. — Norms of atmosphere.
II. — Geometrical corporeal norms.
III. — Physical norms of the materials used.
IV. — Geometrical norms of the materials used.
V. — Building norms.

I. Physiological norms or norms of atmosphere

This involves the means available to us for creating an optimum physical environment for life, through the control of the various forms of energy which act upon the organism and affect sensitivity:

—radiant and luminous energy: radiative forces, light;
—thermal energy: heat;
—chemical energy: qualities of the air;
—sound energy (mechanical): vibrations and sounds.

We also have to be familiar with non-energy factors, that is, with the psychological factors that influence human behavior in a given atmosphere (something like a catalyst or a vitamin for chemical reactions): need for space—sensation of freedom—psychophysiological influence of flowers, noises and colors; influence of magnetic fields, telluric currents, etc. . . .

II. Geometrical corporeal norms

Layouts, cross sections and volumes imposed by Man on each edifice:

a) Principal levels: windows, storage walls, tables, ceiling heights, shapes of stairways and ramps;

b) Passage areas in *cross section:* gangways, doors, forms suited to circulation;

c) *Optimum basic service areas and volumes*, corresponding to the *functions* defined by Team III a—sleep, getting washed, meals, recreation, work—, to the relationships between these functions and to the internal arrangements that derive from them.

III.. Physical norms of the materials used

Here we mean the *characteristic properties* of the materials available to us for building purposes: their nature, their qualities and their defects, their resistance to mechanical stresses, their resistance to destructive agents, both physical and chemical, and their characteristics which influence inhabitability.

These materials are: stone, wood, terra cotta and ceramics, binding materials, steel (problem of stainless steels), reinforced concrete (problem of coffering), glass (problem of insulating panes), aluminum, plastics, various insulators, complexes.

IV. Geometrical norms of the materials used

a) Dimensions of prefabricated building materials

b) Structural stability, and structural dimensions in economic and optimum terms: skeletons, flooring, partitions.

V. Building norms

a) *Optimum surfaces and volumes of the dwelling:*

Normal depths and widths of living cells in housing units, considering the data covered by Team III a on arrangements concerning the dwelling.

b) *Resultant gauges and the consequences they have:*

Dimensional characteristics of housing units.

Problems of orientation and of vertical transport.

c) *Building norms for complex elements:*

Circulatory system (pipes).

Organic equipment (plumbing, kitchen units, etc.).

TEAM III c.

INDUSTRIALIZATION

Necessity of this study

The state of French building was notoriously inadequate even before this war.

The destruction that is still going on has worsened the problem of bringing it up to date.

That problem will have to be solved effectively within a short period of time and under economical conditions both from the financial standpoint and from that of transportation, whether of materials or labor. The result should be quality building, i.e., building which meets the various needs of its future inhabitants as completely as possible.

The job of the *Equipment* Team will be to identify these several needs clearly.

Now, the building methods in use at this time make construction a slow and costly process because they waste labor, materials and transportation, and the quality of what is built is very uneven (any handicraft type of production caught up in a price-war system necessarily produces badly).

This means that there is a fundamental problem:

It is probable that if the methods that have been satisfactorily tested in industry were used, they would make it possible to achieve the necessary goals:

quality, rapidity, economy.

160

It is essential to indicate just how this industrialization should be carried out in order to be effective.

Purpose of the study:

1. Discover just what advantages can be expected from a change in building methods.

2. Analyze the difficulties to be overcome.

3. Outline the proposed organization:

different types of industrialized construction,

industries to be created,

professions which will have to alter their work methods: architects, contractors.

Proposed summary

A. Analysis of present building methods:

—Role of the architect, studies, plans.

—Factory-produced elements.

—Worksites. Contractor's role.

—Transportation.

Conclusion: critical study of a cost price; weak points.

B. Definition of industrialized building:

—"Mass production" building.

—"Standardized" building.

—Construction qualities.

—Qualities from occupant's viewpoint. Aspect.

—Price of French, foreign prototypes.

—Difficulties in moving onto an industrial scale.

—Forecasts as to cost prices, time . . .

C. Proposed method:

—Thorough study:

prototypes of cells,

standardized elements,

Architect's role. Plans.

—Prefabrication industries:

notions about the various categories of industry concerned,

likely raw materials,

brief indication of the type of elements which it should be planned to manufacture,

size of the desirable industries.

—Assembly methods.

Contracting firms.

TEAM IV

HEALTH

Preliminary draft classification of studies to be made
(Headings and chapters of the Team IV book)

Foreword

1. Reminder of the human biological constants which condition the harmonious relationships between man and his external environment.

2. Fundamental directives that stem from that, with respect to building: it is these natural laws which dictate the plans. They must be included in the plans for any building. (Danger of the artificial.)

3. Cooperation between the hygiene specialist and the doctor, on the one hand, and the builders. How to achieve it. Scope of the questions that arise; those to which an answer can already be given here. Opening of a permanent questionnaire to deal with the questions that are still debated or are not very well known.

Outline of the book

The problems will necessarily have to be looked at from various standpoints but, taken together, they should form a coherent clearly arranged whole that anyone can easily consult. Documents will be confined to what is essential. Imperative, unquestionable commandments with respect to building should emerge distinctly.

The most important headings will cover the natural elements which are of prime importance, indispensable to life, such as *Air* and *Light*. Next, another heading, covering *Sound* and the various types of rays; the ways they influence man's health (still in terms of building) will have to be defined and stated. These various elements, in the initial chapter, will be considered at first in the pure state, so to speak.

The *human needs* (satisfaction of optimum psychophysiological conditions) will be the topic of the second chapter.

The multiple effects of the harmonious relationship between man and the environment in which he lives take the concrete form of human needs; some of these are essential and must always be satisfied, everywhere, while others are more peculiar to a specific place or period. Thanks to the achievements of science, technical progress is writing new headings every day to improved ways of satisfying those needs. For instance, study will be made of certain rather more complex problems about the relationships between man and the natural elements: need for pure air of a given temperature and a given humidity content, struggle against the cold, heating whatever is built, struggle against heat, dryness, humidity, etc. . . . problem of lighting in the home by both natural and artificial means, human needs in relation to the various climates.

Then it will be time to make a closer examination of things, looking at man as he is really installed in his life, so as to fulfill each of the four essential functions—

Inhabiting,

Working,

Cultivating body and mind,

Moving about,

as adequately as possible.

Ample room will be given to the still more subtle problems; under the previous headings, their basic elements will already have been taken up but closer attention to details will be needed. For the time being, we are deliberately leaving them under the temporary heading, Miscellaneous appendices.

The natural elements: the environment

A. Air

Composition of the air: pure air (elementary gases and compound gases; ozone).

Polluted air: smoke (different types), poisonous gases, dust, microbes, etc. . . . (analyses).

Hygrometry: humidity, fog, etc. . . .

Atmospheric pressure.

Air and areas covered with green plants.

Air and radioactivity.

(The techniques having to do with air are considered under Chapter II: Human needs.)

B. Light

Studies on solar radiations (infrared and ultraviolet) and other elements.

Various effects of light on the human organism.

Air and light.

Colors: psychophysiological effects (temperaments).

C. Sound

Noise.

Silence.

(Effects on the organism.)

D. Atmospheric electricity.

Ionization.

Electro-magnetic field.

E. Various types of radiation.
Cosmic rays.
Tellurian rays as such.
Vegetative, animal, etc. rays . . .

Human needs

A. Need for pure air (at a given temperature with a given humidity content, etc. The laws of breathing.).
Cubic volume of dwellings (ventilation).
The matter of heating.
Techniques having to do with air (struggle against heat, against cold, dryness, damp, pollution, etc. . . .).
Exact (conditioned) air. Hermetic buildings, etc. . . .

B. Need for light.
Orientation of the dwelling.
Openings: roofs and terraces.
Glass, glass walls.
Problems of artificial lighting.

C. Need for silence.
Soundproofing.

D. Harmonization with the climate.
Various latitudes. Seasons.
The ground (choice of foundations for buildings).
Planted areas.
Horizon, space.
Diverse sites (plains, mountains, seas, rivers or streams).
Winds.
Rain.
Changes wrought in the climate of a place by an urban population center.
Microclimates.
Protection against harmful rays (materials).

Human functions

A. Inhabiting
General relationship between the dwelling and the fundamental natural elements: air, light, space, greenery.
Building materials.
Keeping the dwelling healthy (rubbish and waste, etc.).
General rules on the composition and the internal equipment of the dwelling in order to obey biological laws. (Housing unit, efficient home.)
The city dwelling: population density. Open spaces.
High-rise residences. Collective buildings.
Garden cities. Satellite cities.

(A look at these problems from the standpoint of physical and mental health.)

The rural dwelling (the entire problem).

B. Working

Places of work, factories, offices, etc. (the optimum psychophysiological conditions to be achieved in the various industries).

Prophylactic measures to combat smoke and all artificial sources of harm. (Industrial hygiene.)

Medical care for workers. Relationship between man and machine.

The worker's home.

Work in the country.

C. Cultivating mind and body.

1. Getting in supplies:

Water (the entire problem).

Healthful food.

2. Getting washed:

Showers, baths.

3. Resting:

Bedroom.

Study or workroom.

Vacation.

4. Physical culture and Sports (the entire problem).

5. Sound leisure occupations.

6. The indispensable annexes of the dwelling:

Overall outline (health, sports).

In town.

In the country.

7. School.

D. Moving about.

The four roads. Traveling.

Maintenance and cleaning of public thoroughfares.

Safety.

Miscellaneous appendices

A. The dwelling and the different ages in life (childhood, etc. . . .).
B. The dwelling in terms of specific social functions.
C. The dwelling in terms of the various kinds of human temperament.
D. The dwelling and problems of clothing.
E. Facilities to deal with illness.
F. Facilities to promote health (preventive medicine).

Tuberculosis.

Cancer.

Rheumatism and buildings.

Various pathogenic agents.

Diseases—contagion, etc. . . .

G. Global social hygiene measures.

Legislation. Rules.

H. Permanent questionnaire, including one for the Foundation for the Study of Human Problems.

TEAM V

WORK, AGRICULTURE, INDUSTRY

Working conditions

Moral conditions:

a) lever of happiness;

b) the economists miss the point;

b′) women's role;

Material conditions:

c) the "green factory" and the rural unit;

d) efficient relationship between work, residence and culture (of mind and body).

Moral conditions:

a) The ASCORAL measuring instrument is a certain quantum of happiness, of joy of living. Let everything be organized in such a way that work will not be looked on as a punishment but, on the contrary, as an occupation able, in most cases, to arouse the interest of the person who devotes himself to it.

"Dignification" of labor.

Intensification of labor (obviously, the increase in the products of that labor will be taken into consideration by measures which do not concern us here).

This moral transformation of labor will be achieved by developing the gifts of observation, observation being the factor which determines inventions. Once the creative spirit has been wakened, the worker can feel himself participating in an adventure of which he is one of the active elements. Placed squarely in the modern perspective, that adventure is likely to bring outstanding moral satisfaction.

b) Because the economists are studying material phenomena only, they miss the point, and they will always find the workers facing them, as a mass, taking a hostile or a defensive attitude.

b′) Women's role:

Within a categorically mechanized civilization which has limitless quantities of energy therefore available to it and carries out a fundamental transformation of the means of production, women seem to be in a good position to rediscover their essential role: that of being the guiding spirit in the home. As a result, they will stop working in factories; and, in the country too, through improvements in the panoply of farm instruments and equipment, they will be very distinctly attached to the home once again.

Material conditions:

c) No higher moral level can be reached unless the present resources of architecture and city planning succeed in creating a warm and hearty environment. It is this new point of view which is really the crux of the matter —not just machines and manufactured products any more but also places and premises where living beings devote the major part of their existence—their working lives—to occupations calling for more or less close attention.

And here we are raising the question of the atmosphere in which work is done, a question that was made light of in the first century of the machine age.

In the course of those daily hours of work, that is, of most of life itself, and depending on the measures that will have been taken, psychophysiological reactions will bring forth well-being or the opposite, happiness or un-happiness.

It is possible, in fact it is easy to organize places and premises capable of eliciting favorable psychophysiological reactions. Where industry is concerned, this means *"the green factory"* and, for agriculture, the *"rural* (or *"agricultural") operational unit"* (the farm) of suitable size.

d) Once the atmosphere has been created and arrangements of all sorts lead to efficiency and to a saving of time and effort, there still remains to consider the provisions of a harmonious solar day bringing the varied and necessary periods of rest and stimulus in the weekly cycle and the yearly cycle. Here again, where leisure occupations are concerned, the question of places and premises comes up, and it is architecture and city planning that will provide the solution.

Relationship between industrial worker and farm laborer

a) Confusing the two of them

b) City planning and rural planning

c) Reexamining the way the ground is occupied by industry and by agriculture (linear industrial city and large peasant reserves).

a) Certain industrial and economic circles have raised this question: should the factory worker and the farm laborer be merged into a single entity, a hybrid? (Solution proposed by certain Americans).

The industrial worker is subject to the daily solar law: twenty-four hours, whereas the man who works in the fields obeys a triple solar law: yearly, seasonal, and daily.

It does not seem likely that one and the same individual could be mentally and physically suited to performing both of those tasks, cumulatively; and not only that but also it would seem that the functions which are directly concerned—industry on the one hand, agriculture on the other—would not be satisfactorily performed at all by the work of such a hybrid; the question as raised appears contrary to the nature of things. One problem which certainly is to be faced is that of a type of unity that should reign over all workers, agricultural and industrial, but it seems clear that such unity would be effective on the spiritual level only, not on the material level. It is not the various occupations (labor) that should be merged but the social, civic, ethical, etc. ideals . . .

The deficits of the first machine age stir us to look for that moral unity which is dormant in the awakening of the earth.

There could be another demonstration of unity, once steps have been taken concerning the occupation of the ground, in the form of authentic contact established between the places where industrial activity is carried on and those where agricultural activity is carried on.

Outside of work, the workers of both categories will be able to make contact with one another since such contacts will be brought about and facilitated by the way the places of work—the industrial places and the agricultural places—are laid out.

b) The two terms "city planning" and "rural planning" imply a dualism pointing to two separate events. An urge for unity will lead us, therefore, to look for a third term bringing the two preceding ones into association and appropriate to workers' unity—for which a need is felt so strongly today.

c) *The linear industrial city* extending along the pathways where raw materials are transported will inevitably be located along the major axes engraved into geography and history; at either extremity it will touch similarly inevitable points of intersection where towns and cities have always been located and which were the focal points of the concentration and outward spreading affecting the territory all about. At these points where *linear city* and *radio-concentric city* meet, a large, protecting zone will be set aside, and it is here, in this space-reserve, that the phenomena of reciprocal vitalization between the linear industrial city and the radio-concentric city, or vice versa, (spiritual exchanges) will take place.

Large peasant reserves:

Instead of scattering industries and their specific consequences to all parts of the country, which could give rise to the most noxious effects, the linear industrial cities will encourage the survival of the large peasant reserves whose existence will certainly continue to be good for the country; but when we say "peasant reserves" we do not by any means intend a step backwards nor even the prolongation of a status quo which has recently come to seem a desperate situation (the exodus away from the rural areas). On the contrary; the idea is to animate and intensify the labor of tilling the earth, to invest it with significance by bringing it into harmony with the rhythm of the other industrial activities.

A certain set of phenomena will take care of that. First of all, thanks to electricity, the villages will be endowed with "complementary industries" (the countryside will have been industrialized beforehand—that is, provided with the mechanical equipment that is conducive to working the land, to raising crops and breeding livestock, and, especially, to specific industries: canning [vegetables, fruit, milk], extracts, wood, breeding, fishing and hunting.

Furthermore, what with modern means of transportation—by road and by rail—and refrigeration, new and living relationships will grow up between farmers (unit of agricultural operations) and the big city residential unit (matter of food supply). These new relationships may have decisive consequences concerning, for instance, the anomalous central market (les Halles) of Paris and, in addition, may bring food to city dwellers in an infinitely more prompt and worthwhile way.

It would be of utmost importance to develop the notion of "complementary" industries, which could operate for the duration of the winter or year-round, seasonally or continuously.

One question needing an answer: will the electric motor and the work-bench be set up on the farm itself or inside the community workshop?

Problems of equipment

A. The farm
B. The linear industrial city

A. The farm

What remains subject to the 3-miles-per-hour rate of speed. And what is, on the contrary, propelled at a speed of 30 to 60 miles an hour (motor-driven on smooth roads).

a) Taking these new conditions into account to determine the proper size of the "farm unit" with its civic center.

The result will be increased production; fewer men will be needed but those who are needed will have to be men of *quality*.

And so rural life will be transformed.

The terms of that transformation obeying the laws of today's life which stem from the new pattern of contact and supervision arising in turn out of the new rates of speed, which have, in fact, upset rural life altogether.

b) Problem of land regrouping (in the interests of more efficient exploitation), polyculture problem carried over from the family level to the community level (greens, fruits, grain, tubers, stockbreeding, forests), sketch of the new rural community or at least of the farm unit.

c) Problem of equipment
—exploitation, ASCORAL peasant norm;
—housing facilities;
—equipment for civic life.

B. Linear industrial city
a) Looking at and interpreting the situation in France, taken together with its near or distant neighbors; i.e.:
—point where various forces originate,
—factors determining patterns of movement,
—form of unity between industry and agriculture to ensure new operating conditions for both and favorable contracts.

b) Formation of the linear city (guided by the concern for "natural conditions").

1) Lengthwise cross section of the city (industrial functions and linkups with cities).

2) Widthwise cross section of the city (residential functions and linkups with peasantry).

3) Harmonious determination of the three functions: working, inhabiting, and cultivating mind and body.

4) The three industrial units:
—basic industries,
—processing industries,
—service industries.

5) The green factory (element of the linear industrial city), description of it and comparison with various experiments: Ford, Bata, etc. . . .

Summary of the viewpoint of the leaders of the French peasantry.

TEAM VI

FOLKLORE — THE HOME AND THE WAY IT IS EQUIPPED

A. What is folklore?

The people's knowledge. What is not official. The science (body of knowledge) of the majority, compared with the science of the most educated people.

Folk products have to do with the way the home is equipped.

a) The folk tool: local expression consisting of a solution or a particular form of technique proper to a given period.

b) The handicraft item: spontaneous expression of a way of living or feeling conditioned by the physical surroundings, the material resources proper to a region or to a human group.

c) The popular work of art: expression free of any solicitation or outside influence; or transportation of sophisticated art conditioned by the spiritual or plastic traditions peculiar to a region or a human group.

B. Conditions essential to its existence.

Economic and political isolation ill-suited to material and intellectual exchanges, imposing use of local resources, requiring a family-based economy indicative of techniques still in a primitive stage.

C. Causes of degeneration.

a) In France, the economic revolutions of the eighteenth century and the technical revolutions of the nineteenth bring about exchanges of all kinds and give rise to specializations; this, in turn, causes centralization and gives the capital an intellectual lead.

b) As a parallel, emergence of the democratic spirit and of art criticism, eliminating two notions at once: that of art for, or worthy of, the court and that of folk art; the art of the dominating class becomes the art of the whole of society — or tries to establish itself as such.

D. Reason for partial survival.

Folk art was the opposite of court art until the eighteenth century, when *country became the opposite of city*. Originally, folk art was an authentic expression, a sign of popular vitality. In our own day, it is becoming a sign of the way country as a whole lags behind city, especially in certain regions whose geographical situation and economic mediocrity shield them from the great movement of trade and industrial or spiritual exchanges.

Preserving Folklore

A. Preserving the monuments of past folklore.

Same status as historical monuments themselves.

B. Proposed distinction between folk products.

a) Those folk products which industrial products can replace more cheaply are doomed to disappear.

b) Those with which industry cannot compete directly (basketry) cannot be offered on the market in sufficient numbers except through the use of methods (standardization) proper to industry.

c) In France, in most instances, works of popular art now seem to be no more than awkward transpositions of sophisticated art; subproducts.

To advocate the maintenance of folklore is to distort the spirit of it. To increase the demand for its products is to doom them to industrialization.

The rural dwelling

A. The cost.

The economics of a rural house are governed by a concern for minimum expense rather than by a *concern with aesthetics*. Whereas, because of transportation difficulties, this used to mean necessarily using the materials that were immediately at hand, the minimum expense requirement can now be satisfied by using materials found outside the region.

B. Matters of climate.

a) Roof and terrace — a roof is not an expression of rainy or snowy regions; it is merely the expression of a technique which has not yet found some other means of keeping houses dry — the sun will determine what a house looks like more surely than rain will.

b) Interregional, international architecture. Gothic architecture and eighteenth-century French architecture; *their subtleties*.

Situating a building while at the same time "tuning" it to its natural setting.

Conditions of a possible renaissance.

1. What seems likely to work against it: finding a solution to the agrarian problem by introducing industrial production methods into the countryside since they alone are capable of increasing output. Likelihood that certain traditionally used building materials will be abandoned, as being too poor: (mud, mud-daubed walls).

2. Factors working in its favor.

a) Near future. The disorganized state of transportation will continue to make the use of local building materials advisable for several years to come.

b) Distant future. The leisure time of tomorrow.

TEAM VII

LEGAL AND FINANCIAL QUESTIONS

Stating the problem

The home: *present state of affairs*.

General dissatisfaction.

a) Landlords: non-profitability of buildings and its consequences, stoppages in construction, maintenance and repairs, etc.

b) Tenants: quantitative and qualitative lack of housing, insecurity of tenure, disparity of rents, etc.

c) Contractors: virtually total halt to all activity, either for new work or for maintenance.

Conclusion of the statement: on both the legal and the financial fronts, a dead end.

The legal situation: because real estate is parcelled out, no overall solution, envisaged in terms of the possibilities of modern technology, can be put into practice. Which points to the need for expropriation and the setting up of a system of collective ownership and management.

The economic situation: the non-profitability of buildings will not, it is thought, come to an end until common law is restored — as the landlords more or less openly demand that it be. Since the reinstatement of common law is an impossibility, new financial and economic solutions have to be conceived.

The means and the goal.

The means: inventory of the constructional possibilities of the building industry as it stands today.

The goal: establishment of an "outline plan" on the basis of present constructional possibilities and of the possibilities for extension of the building industry.

The legal, economic and financial solutions.

Land statutes: individual ownership and management replaced by collective ownership and management, expropriation, financing of the expropriation.

Regulations on construction: capital financing of the construction, various possible types of institution; state supervision, government agency, mixed-economy company, concession, cooperative, specifications, duration of the concession.

Regulations as to exploitation: regulations concerning occupants, legal and technical powers and duties, specifications and maintenance program, financial equilibrium.

TEAM VIII

CONTRACTING

The completion of the cycle of ideas brought up by the ASCORAL movement should be expressed in the material realization of the work program that emerges from a study of the problem. This, in fact, is the whole object of the study, and it can be summed up in a single verb: "to build."

When this ultimate point in reasoning is reached, decision-making factors intervene which call upon the performer, the person carrying out the decision — in other words, the contractor.

His role is crucial. The contractor must say what is possible and what is impossible; not only that, but he can and he should suggest, offer solutions, guide the decision. His role has to do with technique and economics, since the goal is to improve quality and reduce cost. But above all, he must fit into his real rank, as ASCORAL's overall doctrine has defined it.

The contracting firm has a very broad field of action. First of all, it includes civil engineering jobs; and when it comes to doing these, France has some very competent industrialists whose fame has spread beyond national boundaries. The calibre of their men and their equipment will enable them, when the time comes, to face and carry out the big programs for transforming the country: ports, highways, railroads, bridges, canals, dams, hydro-electric stations, large factories, etc. . . .

The contractor's field of action also extends to what is called "building," and includes two quite distinct types of construction: on the one hand, structures with clearly individualized architecture for clearly individualized purposes (such as stadiums, theaters, libraries, schools, hospitals, administrative centers, etc. . . .) and, on the other, structures designed for residential purposes.

The first type raises construction problems that vary from case to case; we will leave it aside and consider only the problem of construction for residential purposes.

The idea is to see what role the contractor and his firm have to play in solving the problem of housing and this is an appropriate place for emphasizing how important the question is.

Housing is the most urgent and at the same time the most complex of construction problems. Nowhere has it been solved, for experience has shown without a doubt that whereas, under normal circumstances, the average individual can procure food, clothing and whatever he needs from day to day at reasonable prices, the only housing available to him is an outdated dwelling built for a population which had not developed. The conclusion drawn from this was that there must be something false in the entire building economy, since the rents on housing, half the construction costs of which had been paid out of State aid, were still out of reach for too many individuals. At the same time, it was found that in construction, costs rose incessantly whereas improved mass-production methods, for instance, were making it possible to lower the price of a number of products regularly.

From this it was deduced that the process of building for residential purposes should be industrialized, and we consider this reasoning correct.

But one doesn't make a house the way one makes a washing machine or a car. It is not merely a matter of manufacturing. Obviously, mass-production methods should penetrate more and more into building activity, but it will take far-reaching changes in the economic structure in order to open up the market to this type of production. What is involved here is a problem of integration that cannot be solved unless it is tackled from all angles at once. What is needed is a meaningful, authoritative work outline that will have the effect of coordinating the isolated efforts now being made by a great many minds that are concerned with these questions. That is exactly what ASCORAL's goal is, and the role and function of the contractor and his firm within such a group should be clearly stated.

Is the French building industry in a position to undertake the enormous task of reconstruction, even assuming that the necessary materials are available?

Without the slightest hesitation, we say "No" — on the technical level, the French building industry is not ready.

What are its means, then? What are its methods?

There are two categories of firms in France: the individual artisan's initiative and the industrial firm. They differ from one another chiefly in the volume of their respective activities, for both of them have kept their traditional form and traditional methods — and on neither of those has the machine age had much effect thus far.

The object is to house the French people and (always on the technical level which is our concern) give them the minimum of comfort and conveniences that is compatible with the technical advances of our times. This is a problem which has not yet been seriously faced, and we have proof that no traditional solution can solve it.

Streamlining the construction process, industrializing the building process, finally turning it over to the influence of machines — this is the work of a practitioner; this is the work which the future expects of the contractor, the person who carries out the decisions.

We will have the men. We will have the materials. We will build the machines. The technician is in fact the man who ensures that the technical and economic solution to the problem can be found and that it will be found if he is provided with the necessary means.

As the foundation for this achievement, a work and research program should be drawn up. It can already be outlined.

From the economic standpoint, we can lay down the following program:

Choice of the best and most economical construction methods.
Improvement of old techniques.
Developing new techniques.
Trying out new construction methods.
Reducing manual labor.
Assembling and building under sheltered conditions.
Improving the way the work is organized.
Apparatus and machines.
Leverage and transportation devices.
Setting up workshops on the site.
The "factory-site."
Work in wintertime.
Coordinating the different building trades.
Organizing the worksite economically.
Checking up on workers' and machines' output.

From the technical standpoint, a certain number of vital questions should be looked at in detail, from the angle of scientific progress and modern technique. Some of those questions are:

The foundations.

  Assembling elements in sequence.

  Use of prefabricated elements.

  Use of lightweight materials.

  Problem of walls.

  Flooring.

  Filler partitions.

  Choice of materials.

  New materials (trials).

  Heat insulation.

  Soundproofing.

Technical equipment of the home.

  Heating.

  Pipes.

  Metalwork.

  Plumbing.

  Use of electricity.

  Ground surfaces and flooring.

  Paint.

  Inside insulation (as to heat and sound).

  Furnishings.

  Studies of mass-produced elements and how to assemble them.

Lastly, the problems concerning the use to which the construction is to be put deserve special attention.

  Progress of work (forecasts and deadlines).

  Checking up on how the construction work is going ahead, in terms of anticipated costs and actual costs.

  Detailed study of the length of time needed to do the job.

  Study of equipment and machines.

  Analysis of cost price and running costs.

A separate study should cover the problem of building in rural areas.

  Small farms.

  Housing for farm workers.

  Installations for small farmers.

  Rural construction methods.

  Streamlined organization of the building process in rural areas.

These studies should apply, on the one hand, to the construction of individual houses, and, on the other, to the construction of large apartment buildings with communal services.

Composition: *Text is Aster, Linotype*
set by Affiliated Typographers, Inc., New York

Display is Peignot, Typositor
set by John Schaedler, Inc., New York

Printed and bound by: *Halliday Lithograph Corp., Massachusetts*

Design by *A. J. Pollicino*